Eyewitness
PYRAMID

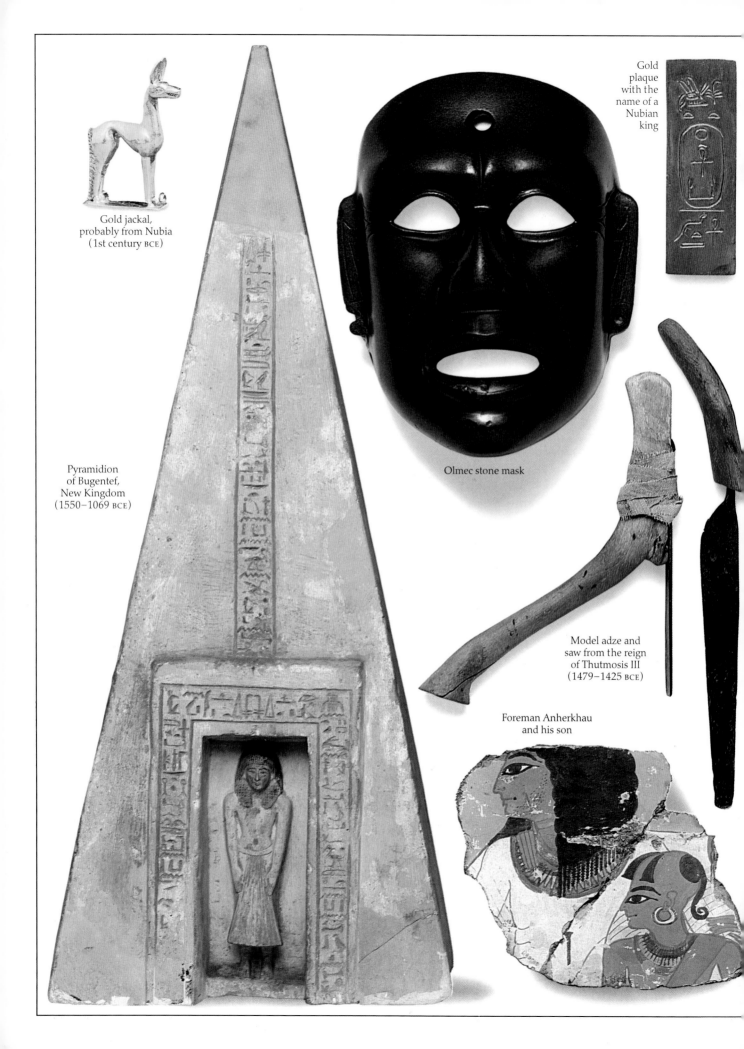

Gold jackal,
probably from Nubia
(1st century BCE)

Gold
plaque
with the
name of a
Nubian
king

Pyramidion
of Bugentef,
New Kingdom
(1550–1069 BCE)

Olmec stone mask

Model adze and
saw from the reign
of Thutmosis III
(1479–1425 BCE)

Foreman Anherkhau
and his son

Bronze
ram-headed
sphinxes
from Nubia

Eyewitness
PYRAMID

Written by
JAMES PUTNAM

Photographed by
GEOFF BRIGHTLING AND PETER HAYMAN

Hetepheres
and her
husband Katep
(C. 2500 BCE)

Two plaques
bearing the
name of the
Nubian king
Aspelta

DK Publishing

Carving from tomb of Ti, Saqqara

LONDON, NEW YORK,
MELBOURNE, MUNICH, and DELHI

Project editor Scott Steedman
Art editor Manisha Patel
Managing editor Simon Adams
Managing art editor Julia Harris
Production Catherine Semark
Researcher Céline Carez
Picture research Cynthia Hole
Editorial consultant Dr. I. E. S. Edwards

THIS EDITION
Editors Lorrie Mack, Steve Setford, Jessamy Wood
Art editors Rebecca Johns, Peter Radcliffe
Managing editors Julie Ferris, Jane Yorke
Managing art editors Owen Peyton Jones, Jane Thomas
Art director Martin Wilson
Associate publisher Andrew Macintyre
Picture researchers Brenda Clynch, Harriet Mills
Production editors Jenny Jacoby, Andy Hilliard
DTP designer Siu Yin Ho
Jacket editor Adam Powley
Editorial consultant James Putnam
US editor Margaret Parrish

This Eyewitness ® Guide has been conceived by
Dorling Kindersley Limited and Editions Gallimard

First published in the United States in 1994
This revised edition published in the United States in 2011 by
DK Publishing
375 Hudson Street, New York, New York 10014

A catalog record for this book is
available from the Library of Congress.

ISBN 978-0-7566-5832-8

Color reproduction by Colourscan,
Singapore; MDP, UK

Printed and bound by Toppan Printing Co.,
(Shenzhen) Ltd, China

Discover more at
www.dk.com

Falcon
jewelry

Nubian pot decorated
with blue lotuses

Jewelry found near the
pyramid of Senusret III
(1874–1855 BCE)

Shabti figure of King Aspelta
of Nubia (593–568 BCE)

Model of King
Khufu's funerary boat

Contents

Tomb model of workers making mud bricks

6
What are pyramids?
8
Built for a king
10
The great Step Pyramid
12
The Step Pyramid complex
14
First true pyramids
16
The pyramids of Giza
18
The pharaohs of Giza
20
The Great Pyramid
22
Inside the pyramid
24
Temples and offerings
26
The Great Sphinx
28
Funeral boats
30
Planning the pyramid
32
Building in brick and stone
34
Tools for building
36
The pyramid rises
38
A slow decline
40
The Middle Kingdom revival

44
Pyramidions
46
Riddles of the pyramids
48
Pyramids of Nubia
50
Pharaohs of Nubia
52
A queen's treasure
54
Pyramids of Mexico
56
Mayan pyramids
60
Aztec pyramids
62
The pyramid lives on…
64
Did you know?
66
Who's who
68
Find out more
70
Glossary
72
Index

What are pyramids?

THE PYRAMIDS OF EGYPT have fascinated people for thousands of years. How did the ancient Egyptians build these massive stone monuments, and why? The most famous pyramids are the three at Giza, near modern Cairo. But there are more than 80 other pyramids in Egypt, and another 100 farther south in Sudan. Each one is a tomb, built by a pharaoh (king) as the final resting place for his body. We know that pyramids were meant to help dead pharaohs achieve eternal life, but we may never know why the Egyptians chose the pyramid shape. It may have developed from early burial mounds, or been a symbol of the Sun's rays or a stairway to heaven. Many centuries later, people in Central America also built pyramids, mainly as temples. Hundreds of these pyramids still lie hidden deep in the region's jungles.

THE GREAT SPHINX
The culture we call ancient Egypt lasted for 3,000 years. The Giza pyramids (pp. 16–17) and the Sphinx (pp. 26–27) were built early on, during the Old Kingdom (c. 2686–2181 BCE). In the Middle Kingdom (2055–1650 BCE), pyramid building was revived. By the New Kingdom (1550–1069 BCE), pharaohs were buried in more secret rock tombs.

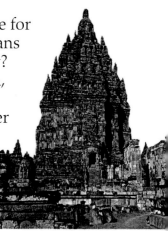

MOUNTAIN PEAKS
Holy buildings all over the world have a pointed pyramid shape. Most culture believe the gods live in the heavens, so earthly spirits can rise from temples to join them. Temples, churches, mosque synagogues, and pagodas usually have spires that rise like mountain peaks. This is the Temple of Siva in Prambana on the island of Java, Indonesia.

BLOODTHIRSTY SACRIFICE
The Aztecs of ancient Mexico built pyramid temples to worship their gods (pp. 60–61). The temples had two staircases, each of which led to a shrine where Aztec priests performed human sacrifices in honor of the forces of nature. They believed they could keep the Sun alive only if they fed the gods with human blood.

Aztec, Mayan, and other Central American pyramids

Egyptian and Sudanese pyramids

WORLDS APART
Pyramids are found in Egypt and Central America. But there is no evidence that the early Americans had any contact with Egypt, or even knew that the Egyptian pyramids existed. In both time and space, the two civilizations were worlds apart.

SPOT THE DIFFERENCE
This is the Mayan pyramid of Chichén Itzá in Mexico. Central American pyramids have flat tops and staircases on at least one side. Mayan priests climbed the stairs to reach an altar on the summit. Unlike the best Egyptian pyramids, which are made of solid limestone blocks, Central American pyramids are filled with layers of rubble.

STONE SUNBEAM
The pharaoh Khafra built this pyramid at Giza around 2530 BCE. It is only slightly smaller than the Great Pyramid, the biggest pyramid of all (pp. 22–23). The pyramid's shape resembles the rays of the Sun shining through a break in the clouds. Its tip may have been cased in gold to make it shine like the Sun.

HIDDEN MOUND

The earliest Egyptian tombs were burial mounds. A simple grave was covered with a heap of gravel, to protect it and mark the spot in the shifting desert sands. Later on, kings and high officials were buried in mastabas, oblong buildings made of sun-dried mud bricks. Some mastabas had sand mounds overlaid with bricks over the burial chamber. This is the Step Pyramid of King Djoser, built around 2650 BCE (pp. 12–15). It was the first pyramid—and the first king's tomb—made of stone.

CHANGING SHAPE

The first Egyptian pyramids had stepped sides, probably to represent a stairway that the dead king could climb to join the other gods among the stars (pp. 22, 47). Later, when the Sun became more important than the stars in Egyptian religion, pyramids were built with sloping sides to represent the Sun's rays. These are called true pyramids. The Meidum Pyramid (pp. 14–15), shown here, was originally built as a step pyramid, but it was later modified to make it a true pyramid.

Some of the pyramid's original high-quality limestone facing remains near the summit

LIFE SOURCE

Every year the Nile River flooded and brought the Egyptians fresh, fertile soil. They believed that the world itself had been created as a mound rising from the primeval waters. The mound shape was thought to be the source of all life. By copying its shape, the pyramid had magical powers to help the king be reborn.

Hundreds of thousands of limestone blocks laid in rows

SON OF THE SUN GOD

This painting shows a pharaoh and the Sun god Re. In one spell from the Pyramid Texts (p. 22), the pharaoh tells Re: "I have laid down for myself those rays of yours as a stairway under my feet on which I will ascend." Re is shown as a man with a hawk's head. On top of his head is the Sun, encircled by the serpent of time. He holds a scepter and the *ankh*—the emblem of life.

Built for a king

THE EGYPTIANS BELIEVED THAT THEIR PHARAOH was a living god. He led the army in battle, passed judgment on criminals, and controlled the treasury. He also represented the unity of Egypt. In early times, most people lived in the north or the south, called Lower and Upper Egypt. It was the pharaoh's role to keep the two regions together. Egypt's centralized government meant he had all the country's resources at his disposal for building his pyramid. The finest sculptors, masons, engineers, and countless workers spent years building the tomb. The laborers who dragged the stones were not slaves. They were farmers who believed that if they helped their king get to heaven, he would look after them in the next world.

Staff

Linen kilt tied at the waist

STAFF OF OFFICE
Egyptian officials were very powerful. Each government department employed large numbers of people, ranging from the chief official to many scribes (officials who could read and write). Officials often built their tombs around the king's pyramid. This statue from 2250 BCE shows an official holding a wooden staff, a sign of his rank and authority.

PYRAMID SITES
There are more than 80 pyramids in Egypt, all on the Nile River's west bank, where the Sun sets. In the Old Kingdom (c. 2686–2181 BCE), pyramids were grouped around Memphis, the capital, near Saqqara. In the Middle Kingdom (2055–1650 BCE), the capital was moved upriver to Lisht, so most pharaohs built their pyramids farther south.

Cairo
Abu Roash
Giza
Zawyet el-Aryan
Abusir
Saqqara
Dahshur
Mazghuna

KEY
▲ True pyramid
◤ Bent pyramid
⬟ Step pyramid

Lisht
Meidum
Seila
Hawara
El Lahun
Nile River

Pharaoh

Nobles and royalty, important officials, soldiers, and scribes

Skilled craftsworkers, painters, sculptors, overseers, and merchants

Agricultural workers and domestic servants (there were few slaves)

THE SOCIAL PYRAMID
Beneath the pharaoh were the royal family, nobles, and important priests, soldiers, and officials. The middle class included merchants and skilled craftsworkers. Most Egyptians were peasant farmers.

SON OF THE SUN GOD
The pharaoh had many official titles, including Lord of the Two Lands and Son of Re, the Sun god. This huge head of Radjedef was found near his pyramid at Abu Roash. The king is wearing the royal *nemes* headcloth. A cobra is poised on his brow, ready to spit fire at the king's enemies. Radjedef ruled for only eight years, between Khufu and Khafra, who built the two massive pyramids at Giza. His pyramid is ruined.

Ancient Egyptian women carried trays and baskets on their heads

HUMBLE SERVANT
Many young women worked as servants. We know what they looked like because model figures of servants were put into tombs so that they could work for their bosses in the next life.

MODEL COUPLE
In Egyptian statues, pharaohs usually have elegant, perfect features. Ordinary people are more natural and realistic. This is the court official Katep and his wife Hetepheres. He has a suntan, but his wife has pale skin, suggesting that she spent most of her time indoors. The statue was found in Katep's tomb near the Giza pyramids.

Hetepheres and her husband Katep, who lived around 2500 BCE

Wig

Her skin is painted a pale yellow

His skin is painted red

The great Step Pyramid

IN THE SHADOW OF THE STEP PYRAMID
For several centuries, important officials built their mastaba tombs around the mighty Step Pyramid. The walls of these tombs are decorated mostly with scenes of everyday life. This carving, from the tomb of the official Mereruka, dates from around 2300 BCE. It shows men carrying offerings of food, including ducks.

T HE FIRST PYRAMID—the first really large stone structure in human history—was built for the pharaoh Djoser at Saqqara in around 2650 BCE. It was designed by the architect Imhotep, who became more famous than the pharaoh he worked for. The Step Pyramid is really a series of six rectangular structures set one on top of the other. Beneath it, cut deep into the underground rock, lie the burial chambers of Djoser and five members of his family. The king's vault was built of pink granite and sealed with a three-ton plug. But it was robbed long ago—only a mummified foot was found inside.

A BUILDER'S SKETCH
This is an ancient architectural drawing, probably made by builders working on the Step Pyramid. The vertical lines allowed them to figure out the exact angle of the building's sloping sides.

BUILT IN STAGES
The Step Pyramid was built around a core of desert stones. Imhotep changed his mind five times as the building progressed. He enlarged the original mastaba form twice before building a four-tiered pyramid structure on top. Then two more tiers were added by expanding the entire structure. It was finally faced with polished limestone to give a smooth finish.

The body of the pyramid is made of small stone blocks laid like bricks

Imhotep

More than 2,000 years after his death, the ancient Egyptians worshiped Imhotep as a god of wisdom. One writer called him "the inventor of the art of building with hewn stone." He is said to have written many books and became a sort of patron saint of scribes (officials who could read and write). He is often shown seated with a papyrus unrolled across his knees. He was also thought to be the son of the god Ptah, whose magic gave him the power to heal the sick.

Bronze statue of Imhotep, New Kingdom period (1550–1069 BCE)

UNFINISHED STATUE
This is one of three unfinished life-sized statues of Djoser found in his pyramid complex. Even in this incomplete state, the king wears a stern expression. The spirit of a dead king was thought to emerge from the burial chamber and inhabit statues like these.

Nemes *headcloth*

Thick wig

False beard

DISCOVERING THE WHEEL
How were the pyramids built? Did the Egyptians have building machines? There are many theories, but little hard evidence. This painting shows soldiers climbing a ladder on wheels. It is the only known image of a wheel from the Old Kingdom (c. 2686–2181 BCE). At that time, the Egyptians did not have pulleys for lifting stones.

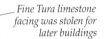

Fine Tura limestone facing was stolen for later buildings

THE KING'S PORTRAIT
The first life-sized portrait in history is this seated statue of King Djoser. It was found in a closed chamber attached to the north side of his pyramid. Two round holes in the wall allowed the pharaoh to see the offerings left by his worshipers. The king is wearing a *nemes* headcloth, a sign of royalty, oddly poised on top of a bushy wig. His eyes were once inlaid with rock crystal. The wear and tear of 4,700 years cannot hide the king's strong personality, seen in his fierce face, prominent cheekbones, thick lips, and heavy jaw.

One of Djoser's names in hieroglyphs

The Step Pyramid complex

HIS LIFE'S WORK
Jean-Philippe Lauer was a French architect and Egyptologist. He spent 50 years reconstructing the Step Pyramid complex at Saqqara. When he began, in 1926, the ruined columns and shattered blocks of stone lay buried in the desert sand. The model on this page is the fruit of his life's work.

THE SAQQARA STEP PYRAMID was just one building in a much larger complex, which also included a series of courtyards and ceremonial buildings. The whole site was enclosed by a massive rectangular wall. Many of the stone structures in the complex are shaped and decorated like earlier buildings made of mud bricks, rushes, reeds, or wood. Though they are carved to look like real buildings, most of them are dummies, complete with fake doors. One courtyard was used for the special *sed* festival, held after Djoser had been king for many years. Crowds from all over Egypt came to watch the pharaoh run a course in the *sed* court. This makes the Step Pyramid the world's first sports arena! By finishing the course, Djoser proved that he was still fit to rule. Then he was recrowned as king of Upper and Lower Egypt on two thrones next to the *sed* court.

KIND OF BLUE
A small underground chamber lies to the south of the Step Pyramid. The king was certainly buried under the pyramid, so this second tomb is a mystery. The carvings and blue tiles may be a copy of the decoration in Djoser's palace at Memphis.

South tomb, a series of underground rooms entered by a steep descending shaft

Outer walls formed a giant rectangle 1,800 ft (550 m) long and 900 ft (275 m) wide

Large south courtyard was lined with beautiful paneled walls

False door, a huge structure that does not open

The only real door

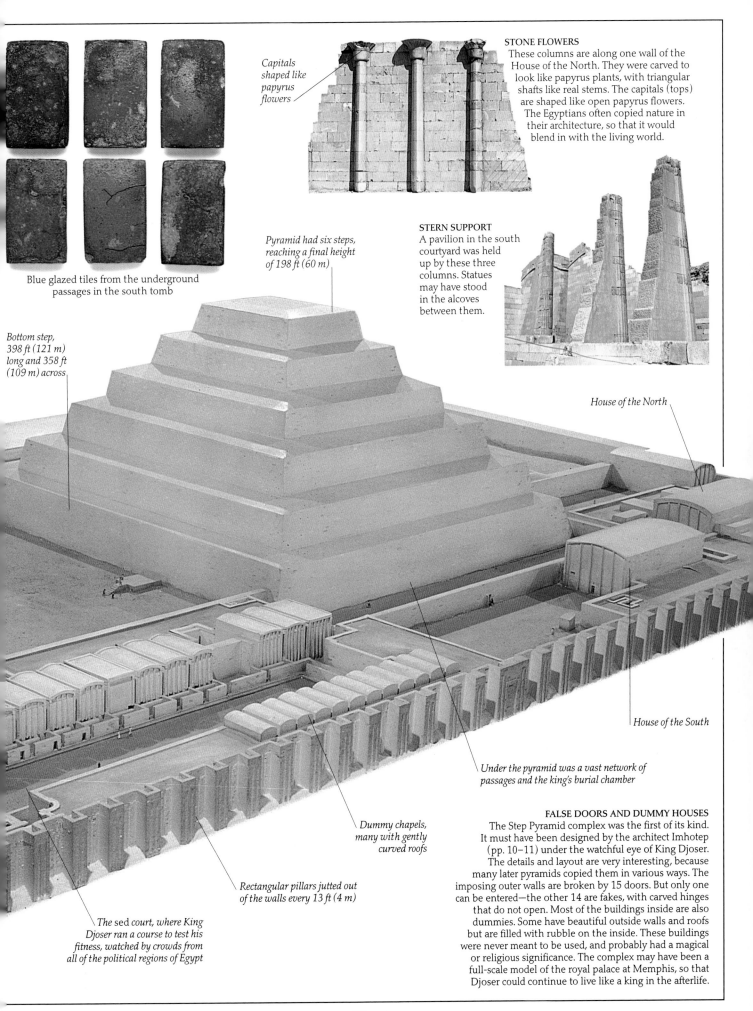

Blue glazed tiles from the underground passages in the south tomb

STONE FLOWERS
These columns are along one wall of the House of the North. They were carved to look like papyrus plants, with triangular shafts like real stems. The capitals (tops) are shaped like open papyrus flowers. The Egyptians often copied nature in their architecture, so that it would blend in with the living world.

Capitals shaped like papyrus flowers

STERN SUPPORT
A pavilion in the south courtyard was held up by these three columns. Statues may have stood in the alcoves between them.

Pyramid had six steps, reaching a final height of 198 ft (60 m)

House of the North

Bottom step, 398 ft (121 m) long and 358 ft (109 m) across

House of the South

Under the pyramid was a vast network of passages and the king's burial chamber

Dummy chapels, many with gently curved roofs

Rectangular pillars jutted out of the walls every 13 ft (4 m)

The sed court, where King Djoser ran a course to test his fitness, watched by crowds from all of the political regions of Egypt

FALSE DOORS AND DUMMY HOUSES
The Step Pyramid complex was the first of its kind. It must have been designed by the architect Imhotep (pp. 10–11) under the watchful eye of King Djoser. The details and layout are very interesting, because many later pyramids copied them in various ways. The imposing outer walls are broken by 15 doors. But only one can be entered—the other 14 are fakes, with carved hinges that do not open. Most of the buildings inside are also dummies. Some have beautiful outside walls and roofs but are filled with rubble on the inside. These buildings were never meant to be used, and probably had a magical or religious significance. The complex may have been a full-scale model of the royal palace at Memphis, so that Djoser could continue to live like a king in the afterlife.

First true pyramids

THE PHARAOHS who followed King Djoser also built step pyramids. The familiar smooth pyramid shape was not developed until the reign of King Sneferu. During his years as pharaoh (2613–2589 BCE), he won wars in Libya and Nubia, and built many new temples, fortresses, and palaces. Sneferu also built at least three pyramids, and he may have built others that remain unidentified. His first, at Meidum, shows how much building in stone had advanced by that time. The construction of the core and outer casing is similar to Djoser's Step Pyramid, but the main structure is made of huge stone slabs rather than many small blocks. The builders had also worked out a new way of roofing the burial chamber, so that it held the weight of the pyramid above, and improved methods of sealing the entrance against robbers. All these features were used by Sneferu's son, Khufu, who built the biggest pyramid of all, the Great Pyramid of Giza. But in total tons of stone, Sneferu's pyramids were an even bigger building project.

PYRAMID PROFESSOR
W. M. Flinders Petrie was a brilliant English archeologist. Over 41 years, he excavated almost every major ancient site in Egypt. He pioneered new scientific methods and published more than a thousand books and papers. Petrie made the first detailed study of the Giza pyramids in 1881–82. Petrie also figured out how the strange-looking Meidum Pyramid had been built.

THE DAHSHUR PYRAMIDS
Sneferu built two large pyramids at Dahshur. This old photo shows the Bent Pyramid, which the Egyptians called The Gleaming Pyramid of the South. It has retained more of its fine stone facing than any other pyramid. The builders started at a very steep pitch, but halfway up they changed angles, probably because cracks appeared. The Bent Pyramid is unusual in having two entrances and two burial chambers—both empty. The other pyramid, to the north, was built later. It is a true pyramid that rises at a very low angle.

PRINCE...
Some of Sneferu's family were buried by the Meidum Pyramid. One tomb held these superb statues of Sneferu's son Prince Rahotep and his wife Nofret.

... AND PRINCESS
The eyes are real glass. The statues are so realistic that when the workmen saw them for the first time, they dropped their tools and fled!

KILLER KING
During its history, ancient Egypt was controlled by a number of dynasties, or ruling family lines. Sneferu was the first king of the Fourth Dynasty. He was an ambitious pharaoh. This carving celebrates a raid on the turquoise mines at Maghara, in the Sinai Peninsula. It shows Sneferu killing an enemy. The text calls him "a great god... who conquers the foreign lands."

FAMOUS GEESE
Sneferu's eldest son was named Nefer Maat. He was buried with his wife, Atet, in a tomb next to the Meidum Pyramid. The walls are painted with colorful scenes of daily life. This famous detail shows geese eating grass. Roasted goose was a great delicacy for the ancient Egyptians.

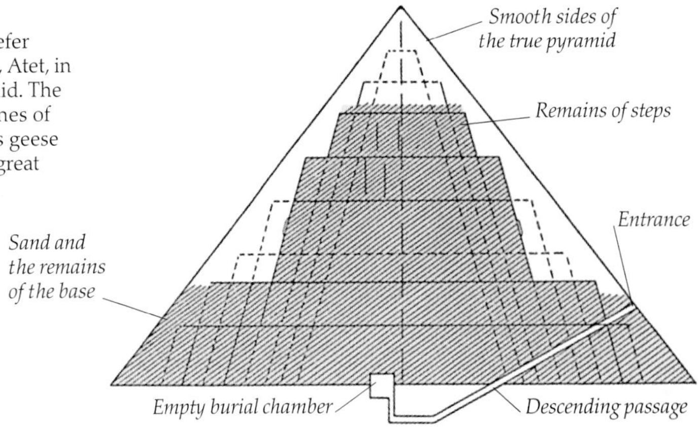

ON THE EDGE
The Meidum Pyramid stands on the border between green farmland, the land of the living, and the desert, the land of the dead.

Smooth sides of the true pyramid

Remains of steps

Entrance

Sand and the remains of the base

Empty burial chamber

Descending passage

AND ON THE INSIDE…
It is usually very hard to tell how a pyramid was made without taking it to pieces. However, the Meidum Pyramid has collapsed enough to reveal its inner structure. This shows that it started off as a step pyramid with eight steps. It was later enlarged into an eight-step pyramid. In a final change of design, the steps were filled in to produce a true pyramid with smooth sides.

DESERT TOWER
The Meidum Pyramid rises like a tower against the desert landscape. Only the pyramid's inner core is left, surrounded by a pile of rubble. This picture shows the causeway leading to the entrance. The Meidum Pyramid was the first pyramid Sneferu built, and it may have been started by an earlier king. It was initially a step pyramid, but Sneferu perhaps decided to convert it into a true pyramid when the Bent Pyramid started to crack. The pyramid's burial chamber was never finished, so it may have been a cenotaph—a memorial to the dead king—rather than a royal tomb.

Top of the sixth step

Fifth step has been cased with fine limestone

Rough underlying stones

Rubble of sand and fallen masonry at the base

The pyramids of Giza

TOMBS BY THE NILE
Like all the major tombs of ancient Egypt, the Giza pyramids were built on the west bank of the Nile River. The Egyptians believed that this was the land of the dead. When the Sun set in the west each day, they thought it traveled into another world where the spirits of dead kings lived.

"TIME LAUGHS AT ALL THINGS, but the pyramids laugh at time." This old Arab proverb pays respect to the great pyramids of Giza, which have sat on a high plateau by the Nile for more than 4,500 years. By the time of Tutankhamun (ruled 1336–1327 BCE), they were more than a thousand years old, and even the Egyptians thought of them as ancient wonders. To the Arabs, who invaded Egypt in 639 CE, the pyramids seemed unbelievably old. From a distance, they are an awesome, majestic sight. Up close, they are massive. The largest of the three, the Great Pyramid of King Khufu, was built around 2589 BCE. At its peak it was 481 ft (147 m) tall, and its sides were 756 ft (230 m) long at the base. It is made of about 2,300,000 blocks of solid limestone, weighing on average 2.5 tons each. Its neighbor, built for King Khafra, is only 9 ft (3 m) shorter. The third great pyramid was made for King Menkaura. It is the smallest of the three, standing only 218 ft (66 m) high.

THE RIDDLE OF THE SPHINX
The Great Sphinx (pp. 26–27) looks east toward the rising Sun. Carved from a huge outcrop of limestone, it has the body of a crouching lion and the face of a king, probably Khafra. Some workers building Khafra's pyramid may have seen the shape in a piece of leftover rock. They probably carved it as a tribute to their king.

King Menkaura's pyramid, built around 2500 BCE

One of Menkaura's three queens' pyramids

Fine limestone and granite facing has been removed over the centuries

The Giza pyramids, seen from the south

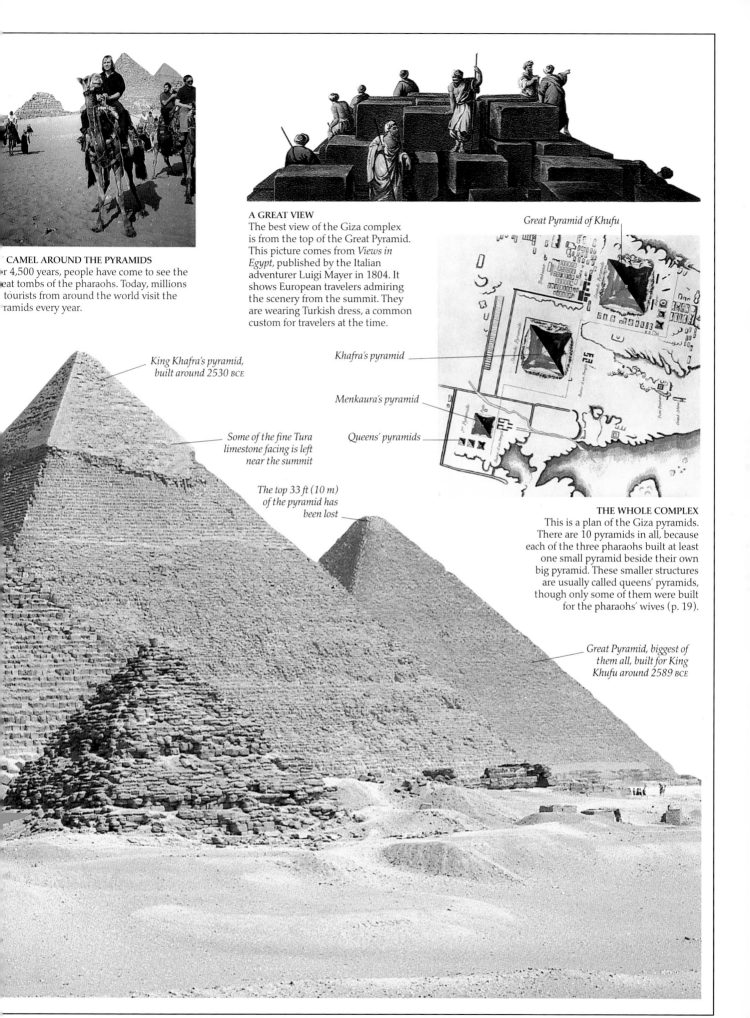

CAMEL AROUND THE PYRAMIDS
[Fo]r 4,500 years, people have come to see the [gr]eat tombs of the pharaohs. Today, millions [of] tourists from around the world visit the [py]ramids every year.

A GREAT VIEW
The best view of the Giza complex is from the top of the Great Pyramid. This picture comes from *Views in Egypt*, published by the Italian adventurer Luigi Mayer in 1804. It shows European travelers admiring the scenery from the summit. They are wearing Turkish dress, a common custom for travelers at the time.

Great Pyramid of Khufu

King Khafra's pyramid, built around 2530 BCE

Khafra's pyramid

Some of the fine Tura limestone facing is left near the summit

Menkaura's pyramid

Queens' pyramids

The top 33 ft (10 m) of the pyramid has been lost

THE WHOLE COMPLEX
This is a plan of the Giza pyramids. There are 10 pyramids in all, because each of the three pharaohs built at least one small pyramid beside their own big pyramid. These smaller structures are usually called queens' pyramids, though only some of them were built for the pharaohs' wives (p. 19).

Great Pyramid, biggest of them all, built for King Khufu around 2589 BCE

The pharaohs of Giza

THE PHARAOH HAD TOTAL AUTHORITY. His subjects thought of him as a god and would do anything for him. Without this absolute power, the pyramids could never have been built. The word pharaoh means "great house," and it originally referred to the palace rather than the king. Khufu, Khafra, and Menkaura had their palaces at Memphis. From there they could admire their massive tombs being built nearby at Giza. The building process took many years—if the pharaoh was lucky, his pyramid would be ready before he died. These huge projects must have put an enormous strain on Egypt's economy. When they were finally finished, the Giza pyramids were given names that celebrated the majesty of the kings who built them. The Great Pyramid was called Khufu is One Belonging to the Horizon. The other two were known as Great is Khafra and Menkaura is Divine.

Pleated nemes headcloth

Royal beard

Pleated kilt

Lion head

Khafra's cartouche

RARE PORTRAIT
Khufu was probably the most powerful pharaoh ever to rule Egypt. Yet the only portrait of him to survive is this tiny ivory statue. When it was found, it had no head. The English archeologist W. M. Flinders Petrie (p. 14) had to sift through mounds of rubble before he finally found the missing head.

LION THRONE
One of the most beautiful Egyptian statues is this portrait of the pharaoh Khafra. He succeeded Khufu as king, and may have been Khufu's younger brother. The statue is carved from a shiny, mottled stone called diorite. The king is shown larger than life size sitting on a lion throne. The statue was found deep in a pit in Khafra's valley temple, part of his pyramid complex. It may have been hidden there to save it from destruction by thieves or enemies.

FALCON POWER
A falcon perches on Khafra's throne, its outstretched wings wrapped around his throat. The bird represents Horus, the god associated with the supreme power and strength of the pharaoh.

HEAD IN THE SAND
The Great Sphinx (pp. 26–27) crouches in front of Khafra's Pyramid. Its massive head is thought to be a portrait of the pharaoh. For most of its history, the Sphinx has been covered up to the neck in the drifting desert sands.

WE THREE KINGS
These are the cartouches (hieroglyphic names) of the three Giza pharaohs. Each name is framed by an oval loop of rope with a knot at the base. The loop represented eternity. By placing his name inside it, the pharaoh hoped to live forever.

Khufu   Khafra   Menkaura

The king has a muscular physique,
while his queen has much softer curves

Menkaura's cartouche

Fine grain of
the stone, greywacke,
gives the sculpture a
smooth finish

WHO'S YOUR FATHER?

Writing 2,000 years after the pyramids were built, ancient Greek historians claimed that Menkaura was Khufu's son. But he looks like Khafra, and many experts now believe Khafra was his father. This painting shows Menkaura as he may have looked in life.

MODEL COUPLE
Most Egyptian pharaohs had many wives, but only two or three were queens, and the king usually had a favorite. This is the earliest known statue of a king and queen together. It shows Menkaura and perhaps his favorite wife, Khamerernebty. The queen is hugging her husband in an affectionate way. Human touches like this are rare in Egyptian art, which is very formal. There are no records about Menkaura from his own age. But Greek historians say he was a fair and just pharaoh. In contrast, they describe Khufu and Khafra as wicked tyrants who forced the whole country to work on their pyramids.

ANCIENT REPAIRS
A broken wooden coffin was found in Menkaura's pyramid. But the style and writing show that it was made nearly 2,000 years after the king's death. Later Egyptians must have tried to repair his coffin after it was damaged.

Queens' pyramids
King Menkaura built three smaller pyramids just south of his own pyramid. None of them was finished, but one is partly cased in granite. This is the largest of the three, where his queen Khamerernebty was probably buried. Many other pyramid complexes include smaller structures known as queens' pyramids. But not all of them were built as tombs for the king's wives. Some were tombs for his daughters, and others seem to have had different, symbolic purposes.

The Great Pyramid

THE LARGEST AND MOST FAMOUS PYRAMID is the Great Pyramid at Giza. It was built for King Khufu around 2589 BCE. Tourists have come to marvel at it for the last 4,500 years. With its original casing of white limestone glittering in the sunlight, it must have been a truly awesome sight. Many people believe it is the greatest monument ever made. The base is bigger than any cathedral's. Until the tallest cathedral spires were erected in the late Middle Ages, the Great Pyramid was also the tallest structure ever built. The precision of its construction is astonishing. The four sides, each slightly more than 755 ft (230 m) long, are aligned almost exactly with true north, south, east, and west. The difference between the longest and shortest sides is only 8 in (20 cm). Inside this mountain of stone, which weighs about 7 million tons (6.5 million metric tons), is a fascinating network of passages, shafts, galleries, and hidden chambers (pp. 22–23).

CLIMBING THE MOUNTAIN
The Arabs used to call the Great Pyramid the Mountain of Pharaoh. In the 19th century, European tourists paid local guides to carry them to the top. This was very dangerous—people who slipped and fell were often killed. Writing in 1875, the American author Mark Twain said it was "a lively, exhilarating, lacerating, muscle-straining, bone-wrenching and perfectly excruciating and exhausting pastime." Today, climbing the pyramids is against the law.

ANCIENT AND MODERN
Giza is now a suburb of the huge modern city of Cairo. This photo shows a Muslim cemetery built next to the Great Pyramid. Khufu's boat museum (p. 29) can be seen against the pyramid. Pollution from cars and factories is damaging the ancient stones. The foundations of the Great Pyramid are shaken every day by the constant flow of buses carrying thousands and thousands of tourists.

Side rises at an angle of 51.5 degrees to the peak, which was originally 481 ft (147 m) above the desert sand

HUNDREDS AND THOUSANDS
The Great Pyramid is the largest stone structure ever built. It is impossible to count all the blocks, so the total number can only be guessed at. At the core is an outcrop of rock that was incorporated into the base. The outer casing blocks were so skillfully laid that a knife blade will not slip between them.

IN THE PYRAMID'S HEART
Khufu was probably buried in the King's Chamber, in the very heart of his pyramid. This room is lined with shiny red granite. It was robbed long ago, but still contains a sarcophagus. This is slightly larger than the door, and must have been put there as the pyramid was being built.

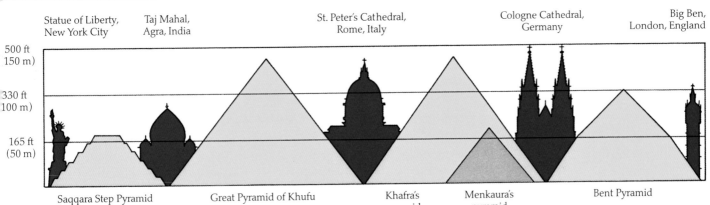

Statue of Liberty, New York City

Taj Mahal, Agra, India

St. Peter's Cathedral, Rome, Italy

Cologne Cathedral, Germany

Big Ben, London, England

500 ft (150 m)

330 ft (100 m)

165 ft (50 m)

Saqqara Step Pyramid

Great Pyramid of Khufu

Khafra's pyramid

Menkaura's pyramid

Bent Pyramid

HOW TALL?

The Great Pyramid is 481 ft (147 m) tall, slightly taller than Khafra's pyramid. This is still taller than many world-famous monuments. But it is much shorter than modern wonders like the CN Tower in Toronto, Canada (1,815 ft/553 m) or skyscrapers, such as the Burj Khalifa, Dubai (2,717 ft/828 m).

CAIRO CITADEL

Huge quantities of stone were needed to build Cairo's many grand buildings and mosques. Some of this stone was taken right off the Great Pyramid.

STRIKING DOWN THE ENEMY

There are only two known images of Khufu, builder of the Great Pyramid. One is a tiny ivory statue (p. 18). The other is this carving cut into a cliff in the Sinai Desert. It shows Khufu killing a Bedouin chieftain with a club. Thoth, the ibis-headed god of scribes, is looking on.

THE LAST WONDER

The three Giza pyramids are the oldest of the Seven Wonders of the Ancient World, and the only one that still survives. The other six—the Lighthouse of Alexandria (right), the Colossus of Rhodes, the Hanging Gardens of Babylon, the Temple of Artemis, the Mausoleum at Halicarnassus, and the Statue of Zeus—are all destroyed or in ruins.

One of three small queens' pyramids

Inside the pyramid

WHAT WONDERS ARE HIDDEN inside the pyramids? This question has fascinated people throughout history. The early Christians thought the pharaoh used them to store grain, as told in the story of Joseph in the Bible. But the pyramids were really royal tombs. Somewhere inside or beneath the huge mass of stone was a burial chamber where the dead king was laid to rest. Since the earliest times, there have been fantastic rumors about the glittering treasures buried with the dead pharaohs. To stop robbers, the pyramid builders hid the entrances and sealed the internal passages with huge plugs of stone. Kings of the Middle Kingdom (2055–1650 BCE) created extra passages and false shafts to try and fool robbers. Despite these efforts, every known pyramid had been looted by 1000 BCE. The few items that have been found were overlooked by hasty thieves. The only intact king's burial ever found belonged to Tutankhamun (ruled 1336–1327 BCE), who had been buried in a rock-cut tomb in the Valley of the Kings. He was lying in three stunning coffins, one made of solid gold, surrounded by priceless treasures. We can only imagine what marvels the pyramids once held.

FORCED ENTRY
The Great Pyramid's original entrance (in the background above) was hidden by casing blocks. Today, visitors enter by a lower hole cut by the Arab leader Caliph Ma'mun in the 9th century.

Two 19th-century engravings of French explorers in the Grand Gallery of the Great Pyramid

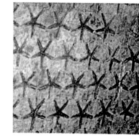

EXPLORING WITHIN
In 1818, the famous Italian adventurer Giovanni Belzoni became the first European to enter Khafra's pyramid at Giza. He was disappointed to find that the burial chamber had been thoroughly robbed. The massive granite sarcophagus was still set into the floor. But there was no trace of the king's body or any treasures.

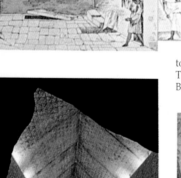

Texts from Unas's pyramid   Stars from the roof   Painted decoration

STARS ON THE CEILING
The burial chamber was at the very heart of the pyramid. The sarcophagus often sat at the far end. The roof followed the angle of the pyramid. Unas's pyramid is decorated with stars and hieroglyphs.

The Pyramid Texts

On the inner walls of King Unas's pyramid are the earliest known religious hieroglyphs. These are the Pyramid Texts. Once brightly colored, these magical spells, prayers, and hymns are about the rebirth of the king and his reunion with the gods in the afterlife. They date from about 2340 BCE, which makes them the oldest known religious writings. Later versions of the texts were painted on Middle Kingdom coffins, and on papyruses of the New Kingdom (1550–1069 BCE), in the famous *Book of the Dead*.

STRIKE A LIGHT

While on campaign in Egypt from 1798 to 1801, the French general Napoleon Bonaparte had his men explore the Great Pyramid. These engravings show them scaling the Grand Gallery, which leads to the King's Chamber. In scale and design, there is nothing like this gallery in any other pyramid. The huge blocks that sealed the passages were stored inside. Over the centuries, the soot from countless torches has blackened the perfectly polished limestone.

KHUFU'S FINAL RESTING PLACE

The King's Chamber is made of granite. The roof includes nine slabs that weigh 55 tons (50 metric tons) each. It also contains five compartments, probably to reduce the pressure from the colossal weight of the stone above.

KHUFU WAS HERE

Some of the rough stones over the roof of the King's Chamber are scrawled with graffiti left by workers. These red hieroglyphs are the only place on the pyramid where Khufu's name appears.

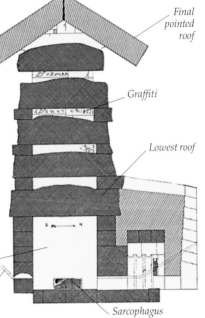

Final pointed roof

Graffiti

Lowest roof

Burial chamber

Ventilation shaft

Sarcophagus

QUEEN'S CHAMBER

Below the King's chamber lies a smaller room that early explorers called the Queen's Chamber (left). However, this room has nothing to do with any queen. Experts now think it was meant for Khufu, but it was abandoned when the plans were changed.

CHANGE OF PLAN

The internal layout of the Great Pyramid was changed several times during its construction. The entrance leads to a descending corridor that runs underground to an unfinished chamber. A second corridor ascends through the Grand Gallery to the King's Chamber. Thin passages called ventilation shafts run from both main chambers toward the surface (p. 47).

King's Chamber

Grand Gallery

Queen's Chamber

Escape shafts for the workers who placed the granite plugs

One of the Queens' pyramids

Entrance

Mortuary temple, where offerings were made

Pit containing a funeral boat

23

Temples and offerings

A TYPICAL PYRAMID COMPLEX included two temples connected by a long causeway. After the king died, his body was rowed across the Nile to the river or valley temple. Here it was mummified—embalmed, anointed with oils, and wrapped in linen bandages. Seventy days later, the funeral began. Priests led the procession, while women wailed and threw sand into the air. The dead king was carried up the causeway to the mortuary or offering temple next to the pyramid. Here, the priests performed sacred rites on the mummy before it was laid to rest in the pyramid. After the burial, the pharaoh's spirit would need regular supplies of food and drink. Every day, meals were placed on an altar in the mortuary temple. Before he died, the king would have set aside lands for the maintenance of a community of priests. Their duty was to maintain the temple and provide offerings for the dead king long into the future.

IN THE SHADOW OF THE GREAT PYRAMID
The Great Pyramid was surrounded by a mass of smaller buildings. Khufu's mortuary temple was built on the east side, where the Sun was reborn (rose) every day. The dead king hoped to be reborn in the same way. The temple centered around an oblong court with 50 red granite columns. The contrast of white limestone walls, a black basalt floor, and red columns must have been very beautiful. Unfortunately, the temple was destroyed long ago. This picture shows the tomb of the nobleman Seshemnufer. Like many important Egyptians, he chose to be buried in the shadow of Khufu's monstrous tomb.

Tomb entrance

LAND OF PLENTY
The spirits of the dead depended upon the living for their survival in the next world. Tomb pictures often show heaps of bread, beer, fruit, vegetables, and geese piled high on a table. By reciting the formula written beside it, the dead person could have a fantastic banquet in the afterlife.

Statue of Seshemnufer

MAGIC DOORWAY
Colorful images of food and drink decorate the
false door of Prince Merib. If no offerings were
left, these magic pictures would come to life.

ESTATE MANAGER
The dead person's
family was often
pictured on the walls
of the tomb. These two
young women holding
ointment jars are the daughters
of Sennedjsui, a treasurer to the
king around 2150 BCE. He ran an estate
where food for offerings was grown. His
titles included Sole Friend of the King.

ANCIENT BOOK-KEEPING
Scribes at the pyramid temple of
Neferirkara (p. 38) kept a detailed
record of all offerings. These
fragments are among the
earliest known writings
on papyrus. They list
daily deliveries of
food, including
joints of meat,
bread, and beer.

False doors and stelae

Worshipers came to pray and lay offerings before a stela in the
mortuary temple. The stela was a slab of stone inscribed with the dead
person's name and titles. In the Old Kingdom (c. 2686–2181 BCE),
it often took the form of a false door connecting the world of the
living with the world of the dead. The door did not open. But the
dead person's *ka* (spirit) was thought to pass through it, so he
or she could leave the tomb and enjoy a meal in the temple.

Magic hieroglyphs

*Falcons represent
the high quality
of the cloth below*

*Stela (stone tablet)
would have been set
up in the eastern face
of Nefertiabet's tomb*

Leopard-skin robe

DAILY BREAD
Princess Nefertiabet
was buried in a tomb at
Giza. She was probably
a daughter of one of the
pharaohs who built his
pyramid there. Her
stela shows the princess
wearing the leopard-skin
robe of a priest. She is
seated at a table piled high
with loaves of sacred
bread. A leg of meat and
a headless goose hover
above the table. The right
panel pictures precious
linen to clothe the
princess in the afterlife.

The Great Sphinx

Winged sphinx made of ivory

FOR MORE THAN 4,500 YEARS, the Sphinx has guarded Khafra's pyramid at Giza. Carved from a huge outcrop of limestone, it is the largest free-standing sculpture to survive from ancient times. It has the body of a lion and the head of a king. The drifting sands buried it up to the neck for most of its history. Attempts were made to clear it as early as 1400 BCE, by Thutmosis IV. When he was a prince, Thutmosis fell asleep under the Sphinx's head after a tiring hunt in the desert. In the prince's dream, the Sphinx promised to make him king if he freed it from the suffocating sand. After he had dug the Sphinx out, the prince recorded his dream on a stone tablet between its huge paws.

HEADS LIKE RAMS
In later times, the sphinx became popular as an image of Amun, the most important state god. A long avenue lined with ram-headed Amun sphinxes once linked the great temples of Karnak and Luxor. This pair of bronze sphinxes comes from Nubia (pp. 48–53).

THE SPHINX'S BEARD
This fragment of the Sphinx's beard was found in the sand beneath its head. The beard was probably added a thousand years after the Sphinx was built. Its surface still has traces of its original red coloring. It seems to have been held in place by a column of stone that included a colossal statue of a pharaoh.

BATTERED AND WORN
The Sphinx was carved from an outcrop of rock that was too crumbly to be cut into building blocks for Khafra's pyramid. Its shape probably suggested the form of a lion, onto which Khafra's stone masons carved an image of their king. The sculpture is about 187 ft (57 m) long and 66 ft (20 m) high. The limestone has been badly weathered over the centuries. The paws were protected with stone facings in Roman times. These were restored recently.

Stone facings added to protect the paws

26

The sculpture is wearing the nemes headcloth, a symbol of royalty

GUARDING THE PYRAMID

Statues of lions often guard the entrances to Egyptian temples. The Sphinx was probably meant to protect the pyramid complex of Khafra in the same way. There is no evidence that it was worshiped in its own right when the pyramids were built. In later times, the Sphinx was identified with Horemakhet, or "Horus in the Horizon," a form of the Sun god.

The Sphinx stands next to the causeway of Khafra's pyramid, looking east toward the rising Sun

In the 15th century CE, Muslim troops smashed off the Sphinx's nose because their religion forbids images of a god

Crumbling limestone, eroded by blowing sand and pollution

BURIED IN THE DRIFTING SANDS

In 1818, an Italian sea captain, Giovanni Caviglia, tried to find a way into the Sphinx. He cleared the sand off its chest and uncovered a chapel. This was one of many modern attempts to free the Sphinx from the desert sands. It was finally dug out in 1925. Many conservationists are worried about the effects of pollution on its crumbling body. Some even suggest it may be safer buried in the sand again!

Stone stela (tablet) erected by Thutmosis IV to record his dream

27

Funeral boats

BOATS WERE THE most important means of transportation for ancient Egyptians. The Egyptians had no wheeled vehicles (except chariots) or major roads—their only highway was the Nile. In their religion, the Egyptians believed that the Sun god Re sailed across the sky in a boat (p. 45). While the pharaoh was alive, he traveled the Nile and took part in state occasions in a beautiful boat. When he died, the pharaoh needed a boat in the land of the dead. In the Old Kingdom (c. 2686–2181 BCE) and Middle Kingdom (2055–1650 BCE), real boats were sometimes buried in pits next to a pharaoh's pyramid. The most famous boat belonged to King Khufu, builder of the Great Pyramid. It is massive, measuring 143 ft (43.5 m) long. In later periods, small models of boats were placed in tombs instead.

SHIP SHAPE
In 1895, two wooden boats were found in a pit near the pyramid of Senusret III (p. 42). Most of the boat pits that have been excavated were empty. The Egyptians may have believed that the dug-out shape provided a magical substitute for a real boat

3,800-YEAR-OLD OAR
The Egyptians did not have rudders on their boats. Instead, they steered with long oars mounted at the stern (back) of the boat. This is a steering oar found with one of the funeral boats of Senusret III. It dates from the Middle Kingdom, around 1850 BCE.

FISHING IN THE NILE MARSHES
This sculpture is in the tomb of Kagemni at Saqqara. It shows men hunting from a reed boat. There are very few trees in the Egyptian desert, so only the best boats were made of wood, which had to be imported from Lebanon. Others were made from bundles of reeds tied tightly together.

Mummified body of a dead man or woman

Flame

Attendant

Incense burner

Boat's prow is shaped like a bundle of papyrus reeds

Eye of Horus (also known as the wedjet eye) was a symbol of protection and rebirth

Sealed storage jar for the voyage

The *Book of the Dead* (p. 44) is a series of spells to help a dead person's soul in the journey through the afterlife. This detail from the book by the scribe Hunefer shows a funeral procession. The mummy of Hunefer is carried in a boat mounted on a sled and pulled by priests. At the front of the procession, mourners wail and throw sand in the air.

Khufu's funeral boat

In 1954, an Egyptian archeologist made a remarkable discovery. Just south of the Great Pyramid of Giza, he discovered a boat pit sealed for more than 4,500 years. Under massive slabs of limestone lay 651 pieces of carved timber. These were put together to make an elegant boat. The name of King Khufu, builder of the Great Pyramid, was written on some of the pieces. It must have been buried by his successor, Radjedef, right after Khufu's death.

Khufu's boat on display in a museum next to the Great Pyramid

Prow, shaped like a bundle of reeds

Five pairs of oars

Canopy

Royal cabin

Stern

Steering oar

Model of Khufu's funeral boat

BOAT BENEATH THE PYRAMID
Khufu's boat had been dismantled to fit it into the pit. Luckily, the builders had made notations such as "fore" and "aft" on some of the pieces. These clues helped the team who rebuilt the boat 4,500 years later. Tests on the wood show the boat was used at least once. This may have been while Khufu was alive, or to carry his body to the pyramid tomb during his funeral.

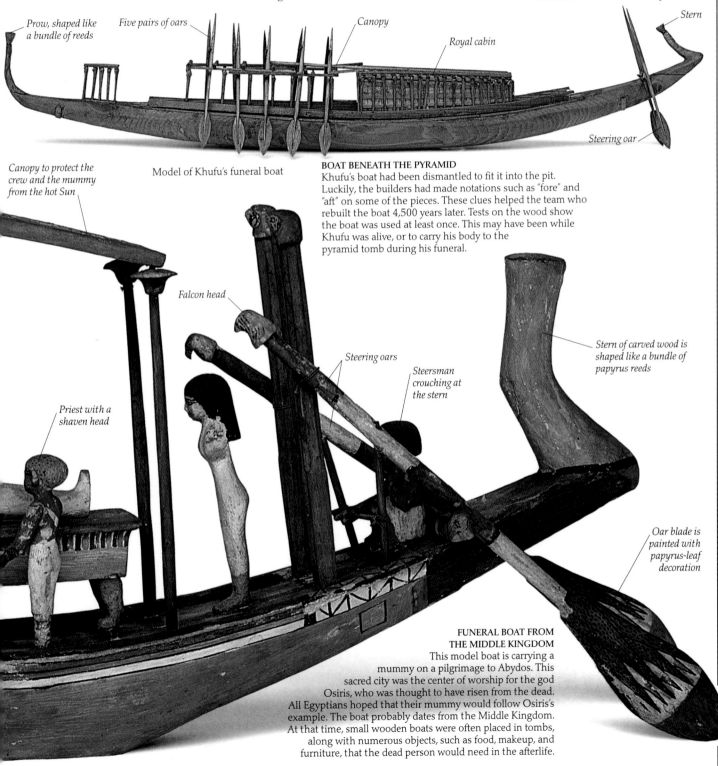

Canopy to protect the crew and the mummy from the hot Sun

Falcon head

Steering oars

Steersman crouching at the stern

Stern of carved wood is shaped like a bundle of papyrus reeds

Priest with a shaven head

Oar blade is painted with papyrus-leaf decoration

FUNERAL BOAT FROM THE MIDDLE KINGDOM
This model boat is carrying a mummy on a pilgrimage to Abydos. This sacred city was the center of worship for the god Osiris, who was thought to have risen from the dead. All Egyptians hoped that their mummy would follow Osiris's example. The boat probably dates from the Middle Kingdom. At that time, small wooden boats were often placed in tombs, along with numerous objects, such as food, makeup, and furniture, that the dead person would need in the afterlife.

Planning the pyramid

THE PYRAMIDS REQUIRED careful planning. First a site had to be chosen. For religious reasons, this was always on the west bank of the Nile, where the Sun set. It had to be close to the river, because the stone would arrive by boat, but well above flood level. The pyramid also required a solid base of rock that would not crack under its enormous weight. Then the site was leveled and true north was calculated, so the sides could be lined up with the four compass points. The Egyptians probably did this by using the stars, since they did not have magnetic compasses. They had set squares and special tools to help them with their calculations.

Pegging the foundations

DIVINE PROPORTIONS
Like sculpture and painting, pyramid building followed a fixed system of proportion. Artists' models like this one show that the Egyptians drew a grid of horizontal and vertical lines to calculate what they called divine proportions. They used small models or sketches to plan large works. Two small limestone models of pyramids have been found. However, there is no way of knowing if these were made before or after the pyramids.

LEVEL PEGGING
This ancient cord on a peg is probably one of a pair used to mark out the foundations of a building. The southeast corner of the Great Pyramid is only ½ in (1.3 cm) higher than the northwest corner. This incredible accuracy was achieved by digging trenches, filling them with water, and marking the level. Then all the rock above the line was hacked away until the foundations were perfectly flat.

Wooden peg

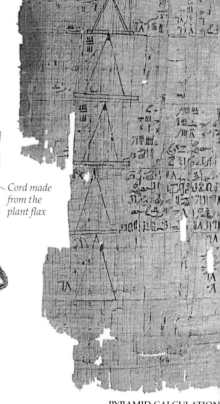

Cord made from the plant flax

GUARANTEEING A TIGHT FIT
Egyptian masons had tools called boning rods to make the stone blocks perfectly smooth. This scene from the tomb of Rekhmire (c. 1450 BCE) shows how these were used. The masons are holding the rods at right angles to the stone so the string is stretched tight. Any bumps are chiseled smooth.

Pair of boning rods

BREAKING THE RULES
The basic unit of measurement was the cubit, the length from the elbow to the tip of the thumb. This was equal to 20½ in (52.4 cm). The wooden rod below is marked in cubits, palms, and digits. There were four digits in a palm, and seven palms in a cubit. The Egyptians also buried ritual cubit rods during foundation ceremonies.

Fragment from a ritual cubit rod made of schist, a hard, shiny rock

PYRAMID CALCULATION
This is part of the Rhind Papyrus, written about 1650 BCE. It shows a series of problems about the relationship between the angle of pyramid and its overall dimensions. The angle of the sloping sides is called the *seked*. It is equal to half the width of the base, divided by the pyramid's height and multiplied by seven.

Scribe is wearing a double wig—his head may have been shaven underneath

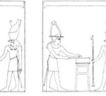

Cutting the soil

Pouring seed or incense

Molding the first mud brick

BLESSING THE FOUNDATIONS

Building foundations had magical significance to the Egyptians. These drawings show a pharaoh performing sacred rites at a foundation ceremony for the Temple at Edfu. This is like the modern custom of getting a famous person to lay the first brick.

CHIEF OF SCRIBES

Hesire's titles included Chief of Scribes and Chief Dentist. This picture of him dates from 2700 BCE, around the time the Step Pyramid at Saqqara was built (pp. 10–13). He is shown with ink wells, a palette, and a pen case over his shoulder. He holds a staff and scepter, symbols of authority, and is seated at a table piled high with loaves of bread.

Scribes are usually shown sitting cross-legged

Hieroglyphic text to secure offerings to the gods for eternity

Ink wells and a palette are slung over his shoulder

WRITING IT DOWN

Scribes (officials who could read and write) recorded the planning stages of the pyramid. On the building site they kept notes of how much stone was used, and which tools each team was given. If a worker called in sick, the scribe wrote down his excuse. This scribe statue of brown quartzite dates from about 700 BCE.

Scribe is holding an unrolled papyrus scroll with his name, Pes-shu-per, written on it in hieroglyphs

31

Building in brick and stone

IT TOOK HUNDREDS OF THOUSANDS of pieces of stone to build a pyramid. The largest slabs used to build the Great Pyramid at Giza, in the roof of the King's Chamber, weigh 55 tons (50 metric tons). Quarrying all this stone and moving it to the site was an awesome task. The core of the pyramid was made from local limestone, a fairly soft rock. But the high-quality limestone used for the outer casing came from Tura, across the Nile. Some internal chambers and passages were made of granite, a harder stone that came from Aswan, 500 miles (800 km) upriver. All year round, gangs of workers at the quarries cut rough stone blocks out of the ground. When the river flooded and rose closer to the quarries, the stone blocks were loaded onto boats and carried to the pyramid site. The teams even wrote their names on the stones—some blocks in the Meidum Pyramid are labeled Boat Gang, Enduring Gang, or Vigorous Gang.

BASALT
This hard black stone could be highly polished, which made it popular for sarcophagi, sculpture, and monumental inscriptions like the Rosetta Stone.

Cartouches (hieroglyphic royal names) of Ramses II, who ruled from 1279 to 1213 BCE

SANDSTONE
Harder than limestone but softer than granite, sandstone was used for building and sculpture. This inscribed tablet, a type of ritual object called a foundation deposit (p. 50), comes from the temple of Ptah at Memphis.

GRANITE
This hard, heavy stone was used for sculpture and sarcophagi (stone coffins), and sometimes for lining passages and chambers inside pyramids. It was very difficult to quarry. An unfinished obelisk is still lying in the Aswan quarry. It weighs over 1,100 tons (1,000 metric tons) and would have stood 100 ft (30 m) tall.

ROWING STONES
Quarries and pyramids were close to the Nile, so the stone could be transported by boat. This carving from the tomb of the official Ipi shows a cargo boat carrying a huge block of stone. The sail is rolled up, so the boat is probably cruising downstream (northward) with the current.

LIMESTONE
The pyramids of the Old Kingdom (c. 2686–2181 BCE) were made mostly of limestone. Because papyrus—the ancient Egyptians' paper—was so expensive, sketches and rough notes were often made on fragments of pottery or limestone. These are called ostraca. This ostracon has a sketch of the god Osiris.

RESTORATION PROJECT
The best Tura limestone was saved for the pyramid's outer casing. Most of these casing blocks were stripped away by later builders who did not want to quarry their own. This block shows the original angle of the pyramid of Unas at Saqqara, built around 2345 BCE, which has collapsed into a heap of rubble. More than a thousand years after it was built, Khaem-waset, Ramses II's son, tried to restore it by refitting the fallen casing blocks.

BRICKMAKERS AT WORK
This painting from the tomb of Rekhmire at Thebes (c. 1450 BCE) shows workers mixing and molding mud bricks.

Straw and sand keep the brick from cracking when it dries

Cartouche

ROYAL STAMP
Mud bricks were often stamped with the name of the pharaoh. This wooden stamp has the cartouche of King Amenhotep II, who ruled around 1400 BCE.

Mud bricks

These were the most common building material in ancient Egypt. The pyramids of the Middle Kingdom (2055–1650 BCE) were made of mud bricks with only an outer facing of limestone. Today, mud bricks are still made by the same process used by the ancients. Wet Nile mud is mixed with straw and sand and pushed into a wooden mold. Then the soft bricks are set out to dry in the burning Sun. The Egyptian word for brick, *tobe*, is the origin of the modern word adobe, a kind of brick architecture.

Mud brick from Thebes, made in around 1000 BCE

A worker leaves rows of bricks to dry in the Sun, in this picture from the tomb of Rekhmire

Tools for building

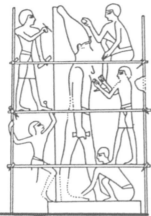

ROCK DRILL
This curved flake of flint is an Egyptian tool from the Pyramid Age. It looks too fragile to work stone. But attached to a wooden pole and spun vigorously with a bow, it became a powerful drill. For a smoother cut, the drill would be used with sand or crushed quartz, mixed with water or a little olive oil.

ALL AROUND THE GREAT TEMPLES, tombs, and pyramids, Egyptologists have found tools left by builders and sculptors. Some of these were lost or broken on the site, but others were left there for religious reasons. The Egyptians believed that a sacred building such as a temple or pyramid had a spirit that would have to be repaired in the next world. So the workers left tools for their spirits to use after they died. The design of these tools has barely changed over the centuries. It is amazing what wonders the builders created with such simple implements.

FOREMAN AND SON
Tools were precious. They were often issued each morning by a foreman who organized his team of workers and locked the tools away at night. This painting shows Anherkhau, a foreman who worked in the Valley of the Kings with his son. It dates from 1150 BCE

HIGHER AND HIGHER
Ancient paintings show that the Egyptians built scaffolding. This detail from the tomb of Rekhmire (c.1450 BCE) shows workers putting the final touches on a statue of the pharaoh. They are standing on a network of light poles lashed together with knots of plant rope.

POLISHING IT UP
After a block of stone had been roughly cut and shaped, it might be burnished (rubbed down with a smooth stone) to give it a polished surface.

Copper

Bronze

MASON'S MALLET
For thousands of years, masons all over the world have hit their chisels with mallets (wooden hammers). This one is made of very hard wood

HARD ROCK
Most stones are too hard to be worked with copper tools. Instead, they were quarried with pieces of dolerite, a very hard rock. This pounder is made of softer granite.

CHISELS
Masons work stone with chisels. These bronze and copper chisels were used to create fine details. The tips could be heated to make them cut better.

Wide dovetail end was pushed into a recess in the stone and stuck there with plaster or mortar

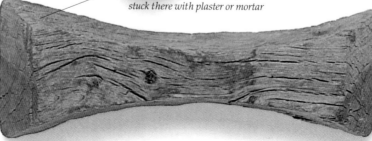

BUTTERFLY CLAMP
Clamps were used to hold blocks of stone together. The wide ends were plastered into holes in the two stones. Many clamps are inscribed with the cartouche (hieroglyphic name of the royal builder)

GETTING THE AX

Axes were used as weapons of war all over the ancient world. They were also good for chopping wood, or to show the owner's power. This ceremonial ax was found in the foundations of a temple.

Hieroglyphs with a cartouche of the pharaoh Thutmosis III, who ruled from 1479 to 1425 BCE

Furniture maker hitting a chisel with a wooden mallet

FOR CUTTING (NOT SHAVING)

The adze was an ancient carpenter's favorite tool. Many paintings show workers chopping and planing wood with adzes. This one from around 1400 BCE is unusual because the carpenter is unshaven with scruffy hair. Egyptians are almost always shown with perfect hair and makeup.

Model adze with a wooden handle and a copper blade

Wooden model of a curved knife

Model saw with a wooden handle and a copper blade

Magic tool kit

This ax, adze, chisel, knife, and saw were all found in the foundations of Thutmosis Ill's temple at Deir el-Bahri (p. 41). They are models, not real tools, and must have been put there by the workers in a special ceremony.

Model chisel

Worker cutting with a knifelike saw, from tomb of Rekhmire (c. 1450 BCE)

Wood was very rare in the desert and often had to be imported from Lebanon

Tang, a projection that fit into the wooden handle

Tip is curved up so it will not catch

PULL (DON'T PUSH)

Unlike a modern saw, this ancient tool was designed to cut as the worker pulled it toward his or her body. It originally had a wooden handle, which has since rotted away.

Cutting edge

Blunt edge that rubbed against wood but did not cut

The pyramid rises

N<small>O RECORDS SURVIVE</small> to tell us how the pyramids were built. The only ancient account, by the Greek historian Herodotus, was written 2,000 years later and cannot be trusted. He claimed that gangs of 100,000 workmen toiled for 20 years to build the Great Pyramid. We now believe that about 4,000 skilled laborers worked all year round. This number was swelled during *Akhet*, the yearly flood, which lasted for about three months. Then thousands of peasants left their flooded fields and came to help on the site. There are many theories about how the heavy blocks of stone were lifted into place. Herodotus said they used lifting machines, but there is no evidence for this. It seems more likely that the stones were dragged up a ramp that grew as the pyramid rose.

MUD-BRICK RAMP
Remains of ramps have been found near several pyramids. This detailed drawing is from the tomb of Rekhmire, made 1,000 years after the Great Pyramid. It shows a building block lying on a ramp

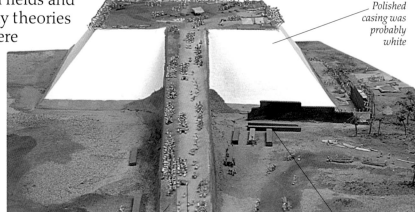

Polished casing was probably white

TWO-WAY TRAFFIC
The ramp was probably strictly organized into up and down lanes. One lane—in this model, the far left lane—is being raised, and is closed to traffic.

Side of ramp being raised / *Stones going up* | *Empty sleds coming down* | *Stacks of blocks ready to be hauled up the ramp*

BUILDING A TRUE PYRAMID
This model shows the most popular theory—the use of one long supply ramp. As the pyramid grew higher, the ramp was increased in height and length. The top of the pyramid was a great square platform, ready to receive the next layer of stones. In the model, the fine outer casing stones are being added as each layer is finished. But some experts argue that the whole pyramid was cased from the top down at the end. The boat is delivering logs for use in ramps, rollers, and scaffolding.

Ramp was quite narrow, and it was always kept at a gentle angle

Teams of men, at least 30 per sled, pull stones up the ramp

BIG DRAG

Wooden sleds with runners were the best way of moving heavy loads. Sleds are quite common in Egyptian art, and several real sleds have been found. This papyrus painting (c. 1000 BCE) shows a funeral procession. Men are dragging the coffin, which is covered by a canopy and mounted on a sled. When moving stones, the workers probably laid logs across the ramp to stop the heavy sleds from getting bogged down in the sand.

UPWARD SPIRAL

Some experts have proposed that the stones were dragged up a system of spiral ramps winding around the pyramid. These could have stood on the casing blocks, or on separate foundations in front of the pyramid. But it would have been virtually impossible to turn the stones around the corners. Spiral ramps would also obscure the whole pyramid, which would make measurements difficult. Making sure the four sides came to a perfect point would have required constant measuring.

CRACK THE WHIP

Romantic drawings and movies often show sweating slaves being driven on by bosses with whips. This is totally untrue. The hard labor was done by peasant farmers. They believed their pharaoh was a god, and were probably happy to help him achieve everlasting life.

Workers add to the height of the ramp

A team dragging a block of stone arrives at the top

Awnings to shelter the foremen and the supplies of food and water

Fine white Tura limestone for the outer casing

Stockpile of local limestone for the core

Teams work on scaffolding to fit the final casing stones on each layer

Work in progress on the entrance to the internal passages in the pyramid's north face

Teams of workmen build the square enclosure wall, which will run right around the pyramid

As the wall gets higher, the workers use wooden pole scaffolding

A slow decline

THE KINGS OF EGYPT'S Fifth and Sixth Dynasties (ruling family lines) continued the tradition of pyramid building. But their pyramids were smaller and not as well built. The largest, made for King Neferirkara at Abusir, is about the same size as Menkaura's pyramid, the smallest of the Giza trio. The kings still cased their pyramids in fine Tura limestone, but underneath was a core of small, roughly joined stones. These have slowly collapsed, so that little more than piles of rubble remain. The cult of the Sun god increased during this period, and many Sun temples were built. These magnificent buildings were places of worship and centers for food offerings, which were taken by boat and placed in nearby pyramid temples.

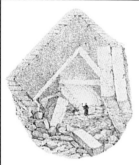

EASY ACCESS
Fifth- and Sixth-Dynasty kings did not make much effort to conceal the entrances to their pyramids. This made it easy for tomb robbers to get in. This drawing shows the entrance to Nyuserra's pyramid at Abusir. It comes from Howard Vyse's famous book *The Pyramids of Gizeh*, published in 1837.

MAGIC HIEROGLYPHS
Magic spells were essential to guarantee the king's survival in the afterlife. These hieroglyphs from the pyramid temple of King Sahura state his many royal titles.

Falcon

FIFTH-DYNASTY PYRAMID COMPLEX
Four kings built their pyramids at Abusir, just south of Giza. This reconstruction shows, from left to right, the pyramids of Neferirkara, Nyuserra, and Sahura. Beyond them are the Sun temples of Userkaf and Nyuserra. The causeway (raised approach) to Nyuserra's pyramid takes a sharp turn, because originally it was meant to lead to the pyramid of the earlier king Neferirkara. After his death, the king was mummified in or around the river temple. Then his mummy was carried up the causeway, and sacred rites were performed in the pyramid temple. Finally, the dead king was laid to rest beneath the pyramid.

LEGLESS NEAR GIZA
Czech archeologists identified the ruined pyramid of Raneferef in 1982. It is in Abusir and dates from about 2445 BCE. This beautiful statue of the king was found in his mortuary temple. Behind his head is a falcon, a symbol of royalty and the god Horus. It clasps *shenu* rings, which symbolize eternity, in its claws. The king was once sitting down, but his legs have been broken off.

Shenu ring in falcon's claws

King is holding the divine mace, a weapon and symbol of royal power

Statue is carved from pink limestone

Top of the king's kilt

ENDURANCE TEST
Despite its name, The Places of Nyuserra are Enduring, this pyramid is just a pile of sand and rubble.

Deshret *crown, worn by pharaohs and the goddess Neith*

Faint moustache, which suggests that the subject is a man

Statue is made of green schist, a hard, shiny rock

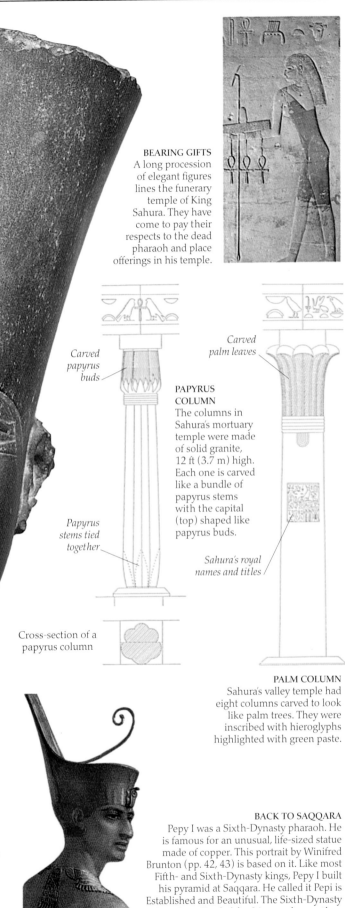

BEARING GIFTS
A long procession of elegant figures lines the funerary temple of King Sahura. They have come to pay their respects to the dead pharaoh and place offerings in his temple.

Carved papyrus buds

Carved palm leaves

PAPYRUS COLUMN
The columns in Sahura's mortuary temple were made of solid granite, 12 ft (3.7 m) high. Each one is carved like a bundle of papyrus stems with the capital (top) shaped like papyrus buds.

Papyrus stems tied together

Sahura's royal names and titles

Cross-section of a papyrus column

PALM COLUMN
Sahura's valley temple had eight columns carved to look like palm trees. They were inscribed with hieroglyphs highlighted with green paste.

MYSTERIOUS PORTRAIT
An interesting legend about the beginning of the Fifth Dynasty is mentioned in a papyrus in the Berlin Museum. In the story, the wife of a priest has three children with the Sun god Re. Many gods and goddesses come to the birth, and the goddess Isis gives names to the three Sons of Re. They were Userkaf, Sahura, and Neferirkara, the first three kings of the Fifth Dynasty. Userkaf built his pyramid at Saqqara. This elegant statue was found in the ruins of his Sun temple, near Abusir. Since statues of kings usually have beards, some experts think it may represent the goddess Neith. But the faint moustache and the statue's location suggest that it is a royal portrait of Userkaf.

BACK TO SAQQARA
Pepy I was a Sixth-Dynasty pharaoh. He is famous for an unusual, life-sized statue made of copper. This portrait by Winifred Brunton (pp. 42, 43) is based on it. Like most Fifth- and Sixth-Dynasty kings, Pepy I built his pyramid at Saqqara. He called it Pepi is Established and Beautiful. The Sixth-Dynasty king Pepy II ruled for 94 years, longer than any other pharaoh. Soon after his death, around 2184 BCE, the Old Kingdom collapsed. It would be more than 200 years before another true pyramid was built.

The Middle Kingdom revival

AFTER A LONG PERIOD OF DISORDER and civil war, Egypt was reunited around 2055 BCE. The period that followed, until 1650 BCE, is called the Middle Kingdom. Strong kings expanded the empire and revived the tradition of pyramid building. They were inspired by the great pyramids of the Old Kingdom (c. 2686–2181 BCE) and often built their tombs near the old sites. But the Middle Kingdom pyramids do not have the same grandeur. They were usually based around a core of mud bricks, which slowly collapsed over the years. Middle Kingdom pharaohs went to great efforts to create complicated devices and false passages to stop thieves from finding their burial chambers. But the kings were buried with priceless treasures, and the robbers stopped at nothing. Despite the elaborate precautions, all the pyramids were robbed in the period of unrest that followed the end of the Middle Kingdom, around 1650 BCE.

Red crown of Lower Egypt

Statue is made of 16 pieces of carefully jointed cedar wood

Long scepter in the shape of a shepherd's crook

Short kilt

SENUSRET II
This colorful piece of gold jewelry bears the cartouche (hieroglyphic name) of Senusret II. It was part of a treasure found in the tomb of the princess Sat-Hathor III at Dahshur. Senusret II built his pyramid at El Lahun, near the Faiyum oasis.

STRIDING KING
Amenemhat I was the first Middle Kingdom king to have a true pyramid. He built it at Lisht and called it Amenemhat is High and Beautiful. His son, Senusret I, also chose to be buried at Lisht. This is one of two statues of Senusret I found near his pyramid. He is wearing the red crown of Lower Egypt; the other figure wears the white crown of Upper Egypt. Around his pyramid were 10 smaller pyramids, in which his favorite queens and daughters were buried.

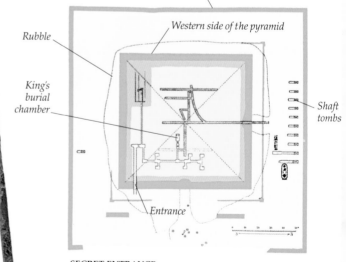

Wall of the pyramid enclosure

Western side of the pyramid

Rubble

King's burial chamber

Shaft tombs

Entrance

SECRET ENTRANCE
This is a plan of Amenemhat III's first pyramid, at Dahshur (pp. 42, 43). It had a concealed entrance and a maze of passages and false doors. Recent excavations have revealed even more inner rooms.

HOLY OF HOLIES
In her own era, Hatshepsut
was famous for her radiant
beauty. The ancient Egyptians
called her temple Djeseru
Djeseru, "Holy of Holies."

Great temple at Deir el-Bahri

The first pharaoh of the Middle Kingdom, Nebhepetra
Mentuhotep was one of Egypt's greatest rulers. During
his 51 years on the throne, art and architecture began to
prosper again. Mentuhotep chose a bay in the cliffs at Deir
el-Bahri, near Thebes, for his funerary temple. This unusual
complex had colonnades, a ramp, and rows of statues and
trees. High on a terrace were six shrines with shafts leading
to the tombs of the king's wives and daughters. There were
two more tombs beneath the temple, but Mentuhotep's
mummy or coffin was not found in either one. The whole
complex is badly preserved. It has been overshadowed
by a similar, larger temple built 500 years later by
Queen Hatshepsut.

QUEEN WITH A BEARD
Hatshepsut was one of the few women
to be crowned pharaoh of Egypt. To
strengthen her claim to the throne, she
had herself portrayed as the daughter
of the god Amun. This scene from
Karnak temple shows her running in
the royal *sed* court (pp. 12–13). She is
wearing a false beard, a sign of royalty.

PYRAMID PUZZLE
Was Mentuhotep's temple capped
with a stone pyramid? For a long time
most experts thought so. But a recent
study suggested that the upper story
may have been a mastaba (flat-topped
tomb) rather than a pyramid.

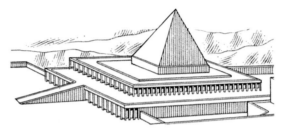

*Red crown of
Lower Egypt*

*Cobras, thought to
protect the pharaoh
by spitting fire
at enemies*

*False beard, worn
by the pharaoh on
important occasions*

EMBRACED BY A GODDESS
Mentuhotep ruled from
2055 to 2004 BCE. As a
young king he reunited
the two lands—Lower and
Upper Egypt—and won
many victories over the
Nubians and Libyans. But
unlike the great kings of
the Old Kingdom, he did
not make Memphis his
capital. Instead, he ruled
from Thebes in the south.
In this fine fragment from
Deir el-Bahri, he is shown
being embraced by the
hands of a goddess.

COLORED RELIEF
The walls of Mentuhotep's temple at
Deir el-Bahri were lined with colorful
paintings. Thousands of broken
fragments have been found in the ruins.
They are now in museums all over the
world. This fragment showing a man,
probably an offering bearer, is in the
Bolton Museum in Lancashire, England.

Continued on next page

FALCON PENDANT
This pendant is made of gold inlaid with the red stone cornelian. It is part of several magnificent treasures of jewelry found around the Middle Kingdom pyramids at Dahshur and El Lahun.

Senusret III

This great pharaoh ruled from 1874 to 1855 BCE. He created a strong, centralized government and conquered Nubia to the south. He built his pyramid at Dahshur. The design of the pyramid buildings and the king's sarcophagus was influenced by Djoser's Step Pyramid complex (pp. 10–13), built 800 years earlier.

Large ears, a feature of many statues of this period

Royal nemes headcloth

THE BLACK PYRAMID
Senusret III and his successor Amenemhat III built their pyramids at Dahshur, just south of Saqqara. This is Amenemhat III's pyramid, often called the Black Pyramid. Like most pyramids of the Middle Kingdom (2055–1650 BCE), it is now just a pile of rubble. The core of mud bricks has subsided over the centuries, and the fine stone facings were plundered for later building projects. The corridors and chambers, including the tombs of at least three queens, were dug about 40 ft (12 m) underground. But the king's burial chamber, with its beautiful granite sarcophagus, was never used.

PHARAOH'S FEATURES
This is Senusret III as he may have looked in life. It is one of a series of paintings of famous Egyptians produced in the 1920s by the South African artist Winifred Brunton (pp. 39, 51), based on careful observations of ancient statues.

Belt buckle with a cartouche (hieroglyphic name) of Senusret III

Pleated kilt known as a shendyt kilt

LOOKING HIS AGE
Senusret III looks stern and thoughtful in this statue carved from black granite. This new, more realistic style of portraiture was introduced during his reign.

Nekhbet, the vulture goddess *Cartouche of Senusret III*

A PRINCESS'S TREASURE
This beautiful piece of jewelry was found in the tomb of princess Mereret near the pyramid of Senusret III. One of the king's victories is symbolized by sphinxes trampling on Nubians.

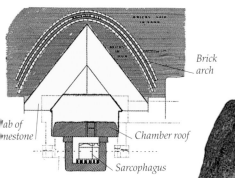

Brick arch

Slab of limestone

Chamber roof

Sarcophagus

THE SECOND PYRAMID

Amenemhat III built his second pyramid at Hawara. His architects built an amazing series of devices to baffle robbers—deep wells, dead-end corridors, secret trap doors, and passages sealed with mighty stone slabs. This is his burial chamber, which is covered by limestone blocks weighing 55 tons (50 metric tons) each. Thieves still broke in, stealing all the king's treasures and burning his body.

Reconstruction painting of Amenemhat III, by Winifred Brunton, 1920s

MIGHTY HEAD
The eyes have been gouged out of this massive head of Amenemhat III. Carved in black granite, it was once part of a full-length statue.

Amenemhat III

The grandson of Senusret III, Amenemhat III was one of the most powerful pharaohs ever to rule Egypt. He built two pyramids and a famous labyrinth (maze) said to contain 3,000 rooms. He is also credited with building an impressive irrigation program. This was an ancient forerunner of the Aswan Dam, with massive dykes and sluices to control the water level of the Nile.

CAPSTONE
In the rubble around Amenemhat III's first pyramid in Dahshur, a granite capstone was found. It is carved with Amenemhat III's royal titles and prayers to the Sun god. The hieroglyphs on this detail read: "Seeing the beauty of Re." Why wasn't Amenemhat buried in the Dahshur pyramid? He may have built it as a cenotaph, a symbolic place for his spirit to dwell. Or he may have decided that the layout wasn't complex enough to fool robbers.

LORD OF ALL LANDS
This is another piece of gold jewelry from Princess Mereret's tomb. By Amenemhat III's cartouche are hieroglyphs that read: "The good god, lord of all lands and foreign countries."

43

Pyramidions

THE MASSIVE ROYAL PYRAMIDS of old inspired private individuals to build pyramid-shaped tombs in the New Kingdom (1550–1069 BCE). These were small brick buildings with pointed roofs capped by a pyramidion, or capstone. They were often whitewashed and had stelae (stone tablets) on the front. Prayers to the Sun god Re were inscribed on the stelae and pyramidions. A courtyard often stood in front of the tomb. This served as a chapel where worshipers could place offerings and pray. An underground passage led to a vaulted burial chamber where the mummy lay. Hundreds of these small pyramids were built on the west bank of the Nile by officials, scribes, and the artisans who worked on the great royal tombs of the New Kingdom.

A PRAYER TO THE SUN GOD
This very pointed pyramidion is made of white limestone. Like most pyramidions, it stands about 2 ft (60 cm) tall. It is inscribed with prayers to the Sun god Re from its owner, Bugentef, who is standing in a niche wearing a wig and an apron. The steep sides are unusual, and are similar to the later pyramids from Meroe in Sudan (pp. 48–53).

The hieroglyphic inscription reads: "An offering that the King gives to Re-Horakhty-Atum (Sun god), lord of the two lands of Heliopolis, that he may give all offerings good and pure to the Ka (body) of the servant of the Sun Bugentef."

UNKNOWN OWNER
There are no hieroglyphic inscriptions on this limestone pyramidion, so we do not know who it was made for. Two of its sides have carvings of the dead person kneeling with hands raised in prayer before an imaginary doorway. This is like the Old Kingdom false door (p. 25), linking this world to the next.

Carving of the dead person praying

Priests
Mummy
Pyramidion
Stela
Mud-brick pyramid

A PYRAMIDION ON PAPYRUS
This painting shows a funeral ceremony taking place before a tomb capped with a pyramidion. It is a detail from the *Book of the Dead*, which describes the journey of the soul in the afterlife. The ceremony shown here is the Opening of the Mouth, performed on the mummy of Hunefer (p. 29).

Nubian captives carrying offerings, including fruits, beads, an elephant tusk, and a leopard skin

SAILING ACROSS THE SKY

All four sides of this pyramidion from 530 BCE are decorated with fine carving. This is the west side, dedicated to the Sun god Re. The ancient Egyptians believed Re sailed across the heavens in a boat, rising in the east in the morning and setting in the west at the end of the day. The south side features Anubis, god of the dead, performing rites on the mummy of the dead man, Udjahor.

Anubis is shown as a dog or jackal

Sun god Re, with the head of a falcon and a solar disk on his head

Boat to carry gods and goddesses through the sky

SACRED SHAPE

This wall painting shows Nubians presenting gifts and food offerings, including incense in the sacred shape of a pyramid. Bread was sometimes baked in pyramid-shaped loaves. The Egyptians worshiped a sacred stone at Heliopolis because they believed that when the world was formed, the rays of the rising Sun had fallen on this stone first of all. For this reason, pyramidions made of stone were also regarded as dwelling places of the Sun god.

Prayer to the gods from the dead person

Maat, the goddess of law and order, with an ostrich feather, a symbol of truth, on her head

Udjahor, the dead person, worshiping

Riddles of the pyramids

CONSIDERING THEY WERE BUILT 4,500 years ago, we know a surprising amount about the Egyptian pyramids. But many mysteries remain. Almost everything has been learned in the last two centuries. A great breakthrough was made in 1822, when the French scholar Jean-François Champollion began to decipher hieroglyphics, the Egyptian picture-writing. By then, the Egyptian language had been dead for nearly 2,000 years. The desert sands had swallowed up the smaller pyramids, and the names of the great kings and queens had been lost or forgotten. Modern archeologists sift through these ruins, searching for tiny clues that will help them to piece together the puzzles of the past. The answers to some questions are still unclear. Exactly how were the pyramids built? And what is the religious significance of the shape? There are many theories, but we may never know for sure.

HOW MANY LABORERS DID IT TAKE?
Experts think it took many thousands of men to move all the stone for the Great Pyramid. Most of them were peasant farmers who worked on the pyramid only during the flood, which lasted three months. Another 4,000 skilled workers were on the site all year round. Their lodgings have been found near the pyramid.

HOW MANY HAVEN'T BEEN DISCOVERED YET?
Some pyramids and pharaohs have only been discovered relatively recently. This gold shell comes from the so-called Lost Pyramid of Saqqara, which lay hidden under the desert sands until 1951. This unfinished tomb was built by Sekhemkhet, a pharaoh who was almost unknown until his name was found in the ruins. Who knows how many other pyramids still lie undiscovered beneath the shifting sands?

WERE THESE TOOLS USED TO BUILD THE GREAT PYRAMID?
When British engineer Waynman Dixon discovered the ventilation shafts in the Great Pyramid (p. 23), he also found two small tools. They are a granite pounder and a metal hook. They may have been left there by workmen. No other tools used on the Giza pyramids have survived.

HOW DID THEY MOVE THE STONES?
There is no proof that the Egyptians used lifting machines, pulleys, or wheeled vehicles. But they definitely used sleds to move heavy objects. One of the best pieces of evidence is this drawing from the tomb of Djehutyhotep at Bersha, from 1850 BCE. It shows teams of workers dragging a huge stone statue. The Egyptians probably used similar methods to move and position the stones when building the pyramids.

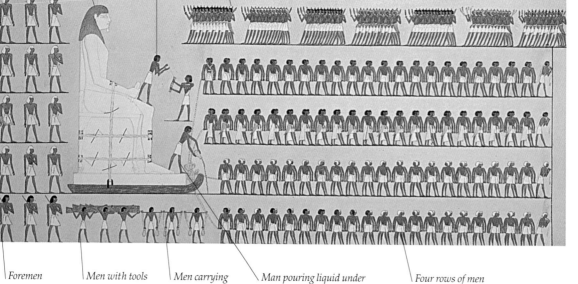

Colossal statue tied to a sled with ropes

Man clapping to keep time

Soldiers

Foremen

Men with tools

Men carrying water or grease

Man pouring liquid under the sled to grease its path

Four rows of men dragging the statue

Mummy case of the lady Takhenmes, Deir el-Bahri, 700–650 BCE

The constellation Orion, including the three bright stars of Orion's belt

Scottish astronomer Charles Piazzi Smyth

Sun or stars?

Many people have tried to explain the link between the pyramids and the Sun and the stars. In 1864, for example, the Scottish astronomer Piazzi Smyth claimed that the pyramids were built to God's measurements. Experts now agree that a pyramid was a symbolic vehicle for sending a dead king's spirit to heaven. But was the king supposed to join the Sun god Re, or become "an Indestructible Star"? The Pyramid Texts (p. 22) mention both. Spell 882 says, "O king, thou art this great star, the companion of Orion…." Perhaps step pyramids were part of a star cult, while true pyramids became associated with the Sun. The thin shafts in the Great Pyramid (p. 23) could represent a transition in belief, since they may have once been aligned with the North Star and Orion. The shafts were probably not for ventilation, but to allow the king's spirit to ascend to the stars.

WHERE ARE THE MUMMIES?
This is a mummy case from about 650 BCE. It has always been assumed that dead kings were mummified and buried in pyramids. But if this is true, why have human remains never been found inside a pyramid burial chamber? Thieves often steal treasures, but in other tombs they usually ignore the dead bodies. Until a mummy is found in a pyramid, the possibility that some kings were not buried inside cannot be ruled out. And if these pyramids are not tombs, what other religious function did they serve?

Wood covered in gold

WHERE WAS QUEEN HETEPHERES BURIED?
The only intact royal tomb from the Old Kingdom (c. 2686–2181 BCE) found so far belonged to Queen Hetepheres. She was Sneferu's wife and Khufu's mother. Her tomb had never been robbed, and included jewelry and furniture and the queen's embalmed organs. But the sarcophagus was empty. So where was the queen's body buried? Maybe at Dahshur, or in one of Khufu's queens' pyramids.

Reconstruction of a chair from the tomb of Queen Hetepheres at Giza, from around 2600 BCE

Lion's paw leg

Pyramids of Nubia

To the south of Egypt, farther up the Nile River, lies Nubia, known to the ancient Egyptians as Kush. This desert land was one of the cradles of African civilization, and was rich in gold and exotic goods. Nubia's position on the Nile gave it great strategic importance, and for centuries Egypt's pharaohs fought to control it. There are more than a hundred pyramids in Nubia. They were all plundered for their stone over the centuries, and today most of them are shapeless mounds. Like the Egyptian pyramids, they were also robbed of their treasures long ago. The first Nubian pyramids were built around 700 BCE, during a brief period when the Nubian kings ruled Egypt. They are at Kurru and Nuri, near Napata, the Nubian capital. When the capital was moved south to Meroe, around 300 BCE, pyramids were also built there. The kings and queens were mummified and buried underneath. Servants were often sacrificed and buried in the pyramid, too, so that they could wait on their kings and queens in the next world.

STEEP SIDES
Nubian pyramids are smaller than the great Egyptian ones and have much steeper sides. Against the eastern face was a small funerary chapel with a gateway decorated like an Egyptian temple. Priests and pilgrims who came to honor the dead king and queen said prayers and placed offerings within the chapel. This is one of the pyramids at Meroe, in modern Sudan, as it appeared in 1820. Some 14 years later, several pyramids at Meroe were badly damaged by an Italian adventurer searching for treasure (pp. 52–53).

God Heh

Dje[...] pilla[...]

Ankh, the sacred sign of life

Scepter, a symbol of power and dominion

STEPPING DOWN
The burial chamber was dug under the pyramid, not built into the structure. It was approached by a long, descending flight of steps, which opened into a series of three connecting chambers cut deep into the bedrock.

GOOD LUCK CHARM
Some pyramids were built around Gebel Barkal. This strange, flat-topped peak was a sacred site for the Nubians, who called it The Pure Mountain. This amulet was found there. It incorporates many magical symbols, including the *ankh*, the *djed* pillar, and a dog-headed scepter. There is also a figure of the god Heh, who represented everlasting life.

A PYRAMID FIELD AT MEROE
These are the pyramids in the northern cemetery at Meroe. They were built between 300 BCE and about 350 CE, when Nubia was conquered by the Axumites. By the first century CE, Meroe was the center of one of Africa's great civilizations. At its peak, Nubia was a fascinating mixture of Egyptian, Greek, Roman, and central African culture. As the kingdom declined, the kings built smaller, less impressive pyramids.

Two small, intact pyramids

The tops of the big pyramids have been destroyed

Painted decoration of reeds that runs around tomb

Log of ebony, an extremely hard, black tree that grows in the Nubian desert

Incense

Lotuses, sacred flowers that still grow by the Nile

Chunks of red jasper, a precious stone used in jewelry

Leopard-skin kilt

EGYPTIAN STYLE
The Egyptians settled in Nubia, founding new towns and spreading their culture. This glazed pot is decorated with lotus leaves in a typical Egyptian style.

GIRAFFE TAILS FOR THE KING
Nubia was rich in natural resources, especially gold. This Egyptian tomb painting shows Nubians giving exotic gifts to the Egyptian pharaoh Thutmosis IV. It was painted around 1400 BCE.

Live baboon

Gold rings

Giraffe tails

Leopard skin

Gateway with two pylons leading to a small chapel

Gold-covered cobra, worn on the king's crown to spit fire at his enemies

Pharaohs of Nubia

Around 750 BCE, when Egypt was weakened by civil wars and disorder, the Nubian kingdom prospered and grew powerful enough to conquer Egypt. For about a hundred years, the kings of Nubia were also pharaohs of Egypt. Succession to the throne was from brother to brother—not from father to son, the usual Egyptian practice. The Nubians were fascinated by the culture and religion of Egypt, and even restored temples there. They also adopted the Egyptian tradition of being buried with *shabti* figures. These mummy-shaped statues, often made of a type of glazed ceramic called faience, were thought to have magical powers to work for the dead person in the next world. The Egyptians were buried with 401 *shabti* figures—one for each day of the year, plus 36 overseer figures with whips—but one Nubian king had as many as 1,277.

Cartouche (hieroglyphic royal name) of Taharqo

Chapter six of the Book of the Dead

One of King Taharqo's 1,070 *shabti* figures, carved from granite

Royal cobra

Nemes *headcloth, a sign of royalty*

Hands hold farming tools

55510

Cartouche of Anlamani

HEAVYWEIGHT KING
King Anlamani (ruled 623–593 BCE) was the brother of Aspelta (see below). This faience *shabti* figure of Anlamani is one of 282 found in his pyramid at Nuri. They were all carved by hand, not made in a mold. The king has a chunky body, with a small head and a huge *nemes* headcloth. His *shabti* is inscribed with chapter six of the *Book of the Dead* (p. 29), a spell telling it to do agricultural work in the next world.

555T2

NO BED
The best-preserved pyramid at Nuri belonged to King Aspelta (ruled 593–568 BCE). This faience *shabti* figure is one of 300 found inside. Aspelta was one of the first Nubian rulers to be buried in both a coffin and a stone sarcophagus. Earlier kings were laid to rest in beds.

The great Taharqo

King Taharqo is the most famous Nubian king. He ruled over Nubia and Egypt from 690 to 664 BCE, at the height of the 25th Dynasty. He is even mentioned in the Bible. Taharqo built many monuments and temples in both lands. His huge pyramid at Nuri was probably inspired by the pyramids at Giza, which he could see from his palace at Memphis.

MAGIC TABLETS
These tablets, known as foundation deposits, have the names of kings written on them. After a ritual ceremony, they were placed in the foundations at the four corners of the king's pyramid, to help it last forever.

Taharqo wears a khat, a baglike wig cover

False beard, worn only on formal occasions

FEATHER CROWN
Taharqo was a powerful military leader. This painting by the artist Winifred Brunton (p. 42) shows him as he may have looked in life. He is wearing a leopard-skin cape and an elaborate feather crown.

The king holds farming tools against his chest

RUINS AT NURI
An English explorer drew this picture of the pyramids at Nuri in the 1820s. There are 20 large kings' pyramids there, plus another 53 smaller queens' pyramids. They were built between about 700 and 300 BCE. All are made from local red sandstone, a soft rock that has not weathered very well. Even 170 years ago the pyramids were in ruins.

Royal cobra

Nemes headcloth

55506

This is Taharqo's biggest shabti, 2 ft (60 cm) tall

King holds a flail and a crook

Shabti figure of the pharaoh Senkamanisken, made of faience, a type of glazed ceramic made with crushed quartz

Shabti figure of King Senkamanisken, made of a stone called steatite

COPIES OF THE KING
King Senkamanisken was buried with smaller *shabti*s than Taharqo, his grandfather, but he had more of them: 1,277 in all. Senkamanisken ruled from 643 to 623 BCE. By the time he took the throne, Nubia had lost control of Egypt.

Shabti figure of King Taharqo, carved from granite

Foundation deposit from the pyramid of King Senkamanisken at Nuri

A queen's treasure

O**F ALL THE HUNDREDS OF PYRAMIDS** in Egypt and Nubia, a hoard of treasure has been found in only one. The pyramid, at Meroe in Sudan, belonged to Queen Amanishakheto, who ruled Nubia in the 1st century BCE. In 1834, the Italian adventurer Giuseppe Ferlini found a magnificent collection of jewelry in a secret chamber near the top of the tomb. At that time, the pyramid was one of the best preserved in Nubia. But Ferlini was not an archeologist. He tore the pyramid to pieces in his greedy hunt for more treasure.

Crown of tall feathers

Cobra

Sun disk

Ram-headed god Amun

Sheet gold decorated with gold wire

ARMS FULL OF BRACELETS
Ferlini found five pairs of bracelets. Nubian queens were shown wearing many bracelets, and Queen Amanishakheto may have worn all 10 at the same time. This is Queen Nawidamak, Amanishakheto's predecessor.

JINGLE BELLS
The queen wore this shield ring to show her devotion to the god Amun. The drop-shaped pendants made a jingling noise, probably to please Amun and repel evil spirits.

Bracelet with a small image of Amun before a chapel

Engraving of a *wedjet*-eye necklace by Richard Lepsius, 1840s

Gold inlaid with colored glass

String of wedjet eyes

ALL EYES TOGETHER
The *wedjet* eye was a very popular good luck charm. It was also known as the Eye of Horus. Egyptians and Nubians wore an eye amulet to protect them from evil. In this necklace, *wedjet* eyes have been linked in a chain, together with a hanging pendant shaped like a lotus flower.

Upside-down lotus flower

SPREADING HER WINGS
The goddess Mut is the centerpiece of this beautiful gold bracelet. She is holding out her feathered wings in a protective gesture. Nubian queens identified themselves with Mut, believing she was the wife of their most important god, Amun.

Goddess Mut

Cobra decoration

Smaller images of the goddess Mut spreading her wings

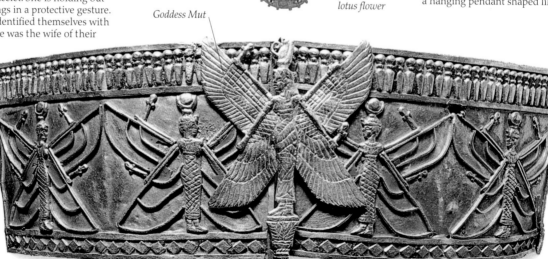

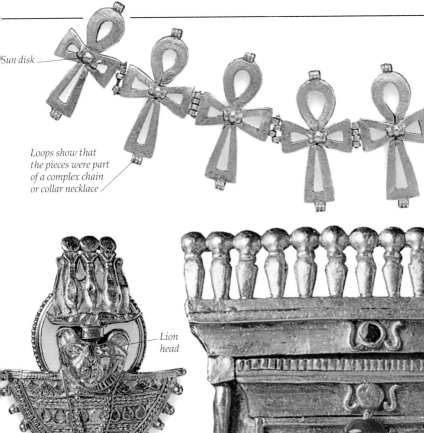

Sun disk

*Loops show that
the pieces were part
of a complex chain
or collar necklace*

*Row of royal cobras
ready to strike*

SIGNS OF LIFE

Cut from a sheet of
solid gold, these eight
ankh symbols form the
links of a chain that was
worn around the neck.
The *ankh* was the sacred
sign of life, which was
usually reserved for
kings, queens, and gods.
Only they had the power
to give or take away life.
The origin of the looped
cross is uncertain, but it
may represent the tie
straps of a sandal.

*Lion
head*

Sun disk

*Design shows the front
of a chapel or shrine*

RAM POWER

This shield ring is dominated by a
ram's head. It represents Amun, the
supreme state god of Nubia. He is
standing in front of a small shrine or
chapel. The gold granules around the
ram's neck form a long necklace from
which a miniature image of Amun
hangs. The name Amun means
"hidden one," and the Nubians
believed he lived inside the sacred
mountain Gebel Barkal (p. 48). In
hieroglyphs, the sign for the ram's
head means power and prestige.

EVERYDAY JEWELRY

There were nine shield rings in
Amanishakheto's jewelry collection.
This one features the lion-headed god
Apedemak. It was not worn on the
fingers like a normal ring. Instead, the
queen must have attached it to her
hair and hung it over her forehead.
Scientific examination has revealed
traces of wear on the queen's jewelry.
This proves that it wasn't made
specially for her tomb. She must
have worn it in her daily life.

Ram-headed god Amun

*Miniature
image of the god
Amun hanging
from the necklace*

Pyramids of Mexico

BEFORE THE ARRIVAL OF EUROPEANS, Mexico and Central America were home to a wide variety of different peoples and empires. Over the centuries, they built thousands of pyramids, usually with steps or terraces rising to a flat top. Most of the pyramids were temples, often arranged in complexes with many smaller religious buildings. Priests climbed the stairs to high altars where they conducted sacred rites, including human sacrifice. A few pyramids were constructed over tombs. Some of the most magnificent structures were built by the Mayan people in southern Mexico between the 3rd and 9th centuries CE. The great Aztec pyramids were destroyed by the Spanish *conquistadors* (conquerors), who invaded Mexico in 1519.

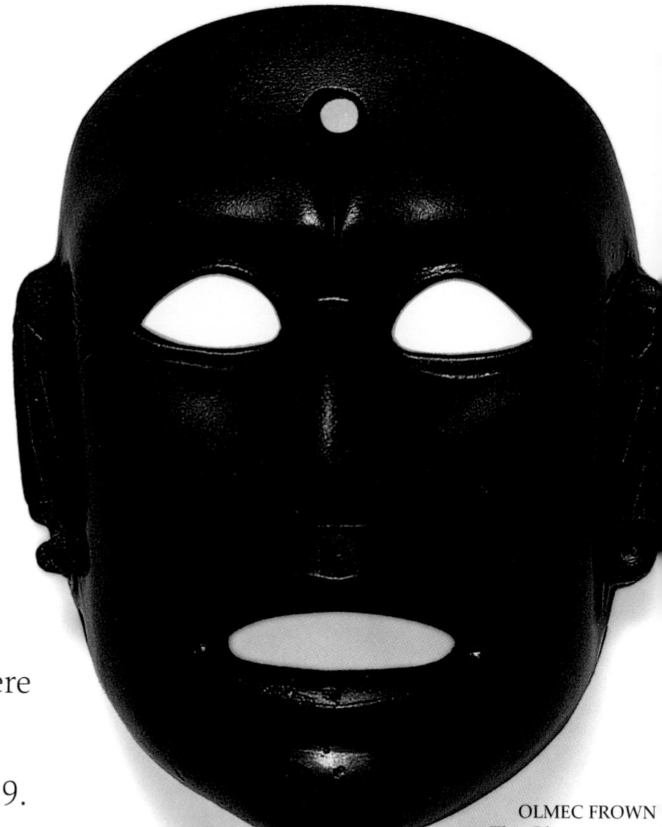

Moche warrior pot from Peru

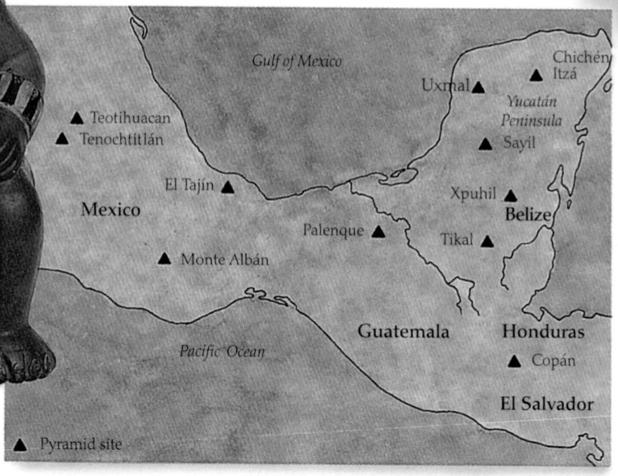

OLMEC FROWN
The Olmecs created the first great civilization of ancient Mexico. They were highly skilled at stoneworking, and built massive earthen pyramid mounds at La Venta as early as 1000 BCE. They also carved beautiful masks as offerings to their gods. The masks have huge features and are usually frowning. The Olmecs' religious beliefs influenced later cultures, including the Mayas and Zapotecs.

MEANWHILE, IN SOUTH AMERICA...
The Moche people of northern Peru built two great mud-brick pyramids, the Huaca del Sol and the Huaca del Luna. In 2006, a tattooed female mummy was discovered in another pyramid, Huaca Cao Viejo. Two years later, remains of 10 pyramids of the earlier Vicús culture were found in Peru. The Moche and the Vicús made fine pots. This pot shows a Moche warrior.

Map labels: Gulf of Mexico; Teotihuacan; Tenochtitlán; El Tajín; Mexico; Monte Albán; Palenque; Tikal; Uxmal; Chichén Itzá; Yucatán Peninsula; Sayil; Xpuhil; Belize; Guatemala; Honduras; Copán; El Salvador; Pacific Ocean; ▲ Pyramid site

THE BIG ONES
This map shows some of the major pyramid sites in Central America. It is not a huge area, but it includes high, cool valleys and steamy lowland jungles. Many sites have never been excavated. For example, hundreds of small pyramids are still hidden in the dense jungles of Belize and the Yucatán Peninsula.

COMPARING SIZES
The bases of the Pyramid of the Sun at Teotihuacan and the Great Pyramid of Egypt are almost the same size. But the Mexican pyramid is only half as high. It is made of 2.8 million tons (2.5 million metric tons) of stone and earth, compared to 7.1 million tons (6.5 million metric tons) in the Great Pyramid.

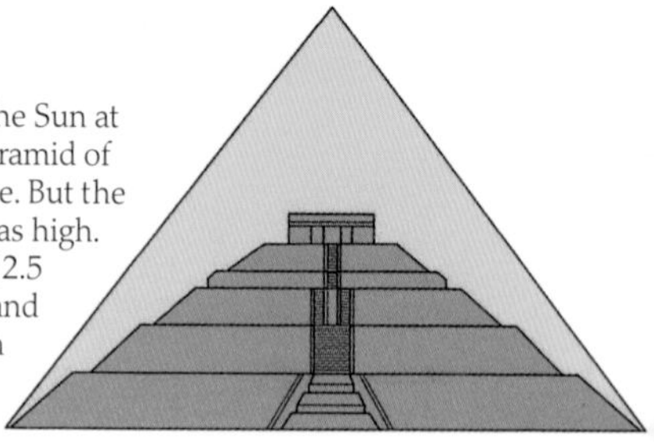

CITY OF THE GODS
Teotihuacan is the most impressive ancient city in Central America. This huge metropolis may once have been home to 250,000 people. Its many buildings and pyramids are carefully laid out on a strict grid plan. The wide Avenue of the Dead runs between the two biggest structures, the Pyramid of the Sun and the Pyramid of the Moon. This is the Pyramid of the Sun, built around 150 CE. It appears to have no internal chambers, although there is a cave inside it. So who built this great city? When the Spanish asked the Aztecs, they said "the gods."

RAIN TOWN
Between 300 and 900 CE, the city of El Tajín, of the Totonac culture, was the most important center on the Veracruz coast of Mexico. This lush area was famous for its corn, cocoa, and cotton. The town itself was named after the rain god, Tajín. This imaginative painting by the Mexican artist Diego Rivera shows two pyramids. The one on the right is the Pyramid of the Niches.

A detail from the fresco *Offering of Fruits, Tobacco, Cacao, and Vanilla to the Emperor*, by Diego Rivera, 1950

A NICHE A DAY
The Pyramid of the Niches at El Tajín rises in six tiers. Each tier contains rows of niches. There are 365 niches in all, one for each day of the year. Offerings or figures of gods may have been placed in the niches.

ZAPOTEC GOD
The Zapotec people made their capital at Monte Albán, in the Oaxaca region of Mexico. Between 600 BCE and 800 CE, they built a remarkable city of pyramid temples and tombs there. The tombs have niches in which clay funerary urns were placed. On this urn the rain god Cocijo wears a typical Zapotec feathered headdress.

Elaborate feathered headdress

Urn was built up from layers of clay slabs

Urn depicts the rain god, Cocijo, wearing ear studs and sticking out his forked tongue

Urn is made around a cylinder that held food offerings or ashes

Mayan pyramids

CITY KINGDOM
The Maya did not have a single capital or king. Instead, each city governed itself under its own ruler. One important later city was Chichén Itzá in the Yucatán Peninsula, Mexico. There were many religious and administrative buildings at Chichén Itzá, including the famous pyramid El Castillo. The stone pillars in the architecture show the influence of the Toltecs, a neighboring culture. People were thrown to their deaths in the sacred Well of Sacrifice.

BETWEEN THE 3RD AND 9TH CENTURIES CE, the Maya built pyramids all across eastern Mexico and into modern Belize, Guatemala, Honduras, and El Salvador. Made of stone blocks held together with strong lime mortar, Mayan pyramids were built at steeper angles than Egyptian ones. The staircases sometimes got narrower as they rose, to make the pyramids seem even taller and steeper. This also drew attention to the rituals performed in the temple chamber at the top. Crowds gathered at the base, but only priests could climb to the sacred heights. The Maya were skilled astronomers and laid out their pyramids according to the Sun, Moon, and stars. They also developed yearly and sacred calendars, a system of mathematics, and their own system of picture-writing, called glyphs. This still has not been fully deciphered.

DANCING GODS
These drawings show two gods shared by most ancient Central American cultures. On his nightly journey beneath the earth, the Sun god became the jaguar god of the underworld. The black spots on his fur symbolized the stars. The serpent Quetzalcoatl was thought to express sacred power. A person's head is often shown emerging from his open mouth, to link this sacred creature to the human world.

Jaguar god

Quetzalcoatl

JAGUAR POT
Very few Mayan wall paintings remain. But we can get some idea of their quality from the decorated ceramics that have survived. Pots for the rich or for religious use were covered with stucco (plaster), which was painted while it was still wet. This one shows a jaguar, an animal admired for its skill in hunting and its strength, ferocity, and cunning.

Temple chamber where priests conducted sacred rituals

Entrance to the temple chamber

Stone was coated with plaster and then painted, possibly blood-red

Four staircases probably symbolized the division of the cosmos into four quadrants

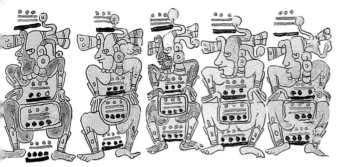

CRACKING THE CODE

For more than a hundred years, researchers struggled to decipher the mysterious Mayan glyphs. Only in the last 30 years have they started to break the code. There are many stone inscriptions. But most of the Mayan books, called codices, were burned in 1562 by a Spanish priest who claimed they were the works of the devil. Only four survived. These were written and painted on bark paper folded in sections. They have helped us to understand the Mayan calendars and mathematics. These five gods are from the *Codex Tro-Cortesianus*. The bars and dots are glyphs for numbers.

FEATHERED SERPENT

The first known god of Mexico was Quetzalcoatl, the feathered serpent. This is one of the seven serpent figures on the northern stairs of El Castillo pyramid at Chichén Itzá. At the fall equinox, around September 23 every year, the Sun shines through the mouths of all seven serpents.

LOST CITIES

In the 800s, the Mayan civilization went through a spectacular collapse. No one really knows why. Ravaged by war and famine, the cities were abandoned one by one. The jungle plants took over the temples and the statues were swallowed by the undergrowth. These lost cities were rediscovered only recently. This is a photo of El Castillo pyramid at Chichén Itzá, taken by an English explorer in around 1900.

Top is 79 ft (24 m) high

STEPPING THE DAYS AWAY

This model shows El Castillo pyramid at Chichén Itzá. It has four staircases, three with 91 steps and one with 92. That makes a total of 365 steps, one for each day of the year.

Single northern staircase on the inner Toltec pyramid

Outer Mayan pyramid has four staircases

INNER TEMPLES

Mexican pyramids were often enlarged by new rulers. In this way, they grew bigger and bigger. In 1930, Mexican archeologists discovered an earlier temple inside the El Castillo pyramid at Chichén Itzá. Probably built by the Toltecs, it also has nine levels, but only one staircase. Inside the temple chamber are a magnificent jaguar throne and a sculpture on which offerings were placed.

Nine terraces

57

Continued on next page

Continued from previous page

Bloodletting and sacrifice

Bloody rituals were a vital part of Mayan life. The Mayans believed that to keep the cosmic order, the gods needed to be fed with blood. In return, the gods would provide good harvests and prevent natural disasters such as earthquakes. One mural shows prisoners of war being tortured by having their fingernails pulled out. Human sacrifice may have been introduced to the Maya by the warlike Toltecs. The victims were prisoners of war, slaves, or children bought especially for the occasion. The priest who performed the sacrifice was helped by four old men who held the victim's arms and legs while the chest was ripped open. The priests performed these sacrifices during special festivals in the sacred calendar.

SPILLING YOUR OWN BLOOD
Mayan nobles mutilated themselves in special bloodletting ceremonies. They passed needles or stingray spines through parts of the body and collected the blood to smear on statues. Men usually pierced their penises. This sculpture from Yaxchilán (south of Tikal) shows Lady Xoc passing a string of thorns through her tongue. The ruler Shield Jaguar looks on.

Glyphs from a wooden beam on the Temple of the Giant Jaguar, Tikal, Guatemala

PUBLIC ADDRESS
There are five major pyramid complexes at Tikal, Guatemala. This is the steeply rising Temple I, also known as the Temple of the Giant Jaguar, one of the most impressive of all surviving Mayan pyramids. The chamber at the top was designed to amplify the priests' voices, so they could be heard by spectators at the base. The tomb of a Mayan lord, Ah Cacan, was beneath the pyramid.

OVAL PYRAMID
The Pyramid of the Magician at Uxmal, Mexico, has curved walls. It was built in five distinct phases from the 6th to 10th centuries. The ceremonial stairway on the west side leads to the broad temple chamber. The entrance is richly decorated, and looks like the mouth of a great monster.

DOORWAY TO DATES
Mayan temple doors were spanned by wooden beams. The wood can be dated by the radiocarbon process. This helps experts to confirm the dates of Mayan history, which still are not very clear. These details from a wooden beam are glyphs.

A glyph from a wooden beam on the Temple of the Giant Jaguar, Tikal, Guatemala

King, wearing a feathered crown

Members of the royal family

Nobles, priests, and warriors

Merchants, artists, and craftsworkers

Peasant farmers, laborers, and slaves

MAYAN SOCIAL PYRAMID
A modern Mexican artist painted this pyramid to show the different classes of Mayan society. It is done in the style of the beautiful frescoes found at Bonampak, Guatemala. Each important Mayan city had its own ruler or king, who was regarded by his people as a living god. To live up to his reputation, the king built splendid palaces and temples.

JUNGLE RUINS
Between 1839 and 1842, American John Stephens and Englishman Frederick Catherwood made two famous expeditions to explore Mayan ruins. Jungle travel was dangerous, and they both suffered bad bouts of malaria. Their writings and drawings revealed the full splendor of the lost civilization. This illustration shows a pyramid at Tulum, Mexico.

MYSTERIOUS GODS
This is a reconstruction of a frieze from Campeche, Mexico. Traces of color suggest that the original was brightly painted. Very little is known about the bewildering variety of Mayan gods.

Aztec pyramids

Tezcatlipoca

Huitzilopochtli

THE AZTECS RULED the last great empire of Central America. They called themselves *Mexica* and made their capital at Tenochtitlán, now Mexico City. When the Spanish *conquistadors* entered Tenochtitlán in 1519, they found one of the largest cities in the world. They were impressed by its beauty, cleanliness, and order. But as they approached the huge ceremonial center, the Spaniards were horrified by the smell of blood. The Aztecs used their pyramids for human sacrifice, which they believed provided vital energy needed for the workings of the universe. In the last years of their empire, thousands of victims, mostly prisoners of war, were sacrificed each year. The Aztecs built their pyramids from a core of sun-dried mud bricks faced with stone held together by mortar. None of them was very high. The tallest, the Great Temple of Tenochtitlán, was only one-fifth of the height of the Great Pyramid at Giza

REPAYING THE GODS
The top of the pyramid was a place of bloody sacrifice. Here the priests removed the still-beating heart of the victim. They then threw the body down the steps, and the limbs were hacked off and ceremonially eaten. The Aztecs believed that the world had been created by their gods' own sacrifice. These terrible rituals were their gifts of thanks.

The snake was associated with the god Quetzalcoatl, whose name meant "feathered serpent"

SACRIFICIAL KNIFE
The victim's heart was cut out with a stone knife. The Aztecs had no iron and made their tools from razor-sharp flint or obsidian, a volcanic glass. This flint blade is decorated with a turquoise mosaic of a snake, a symbol of sacred power. The Aztecs excelled at mosaic work using jade, coral, shell, and turquoise.

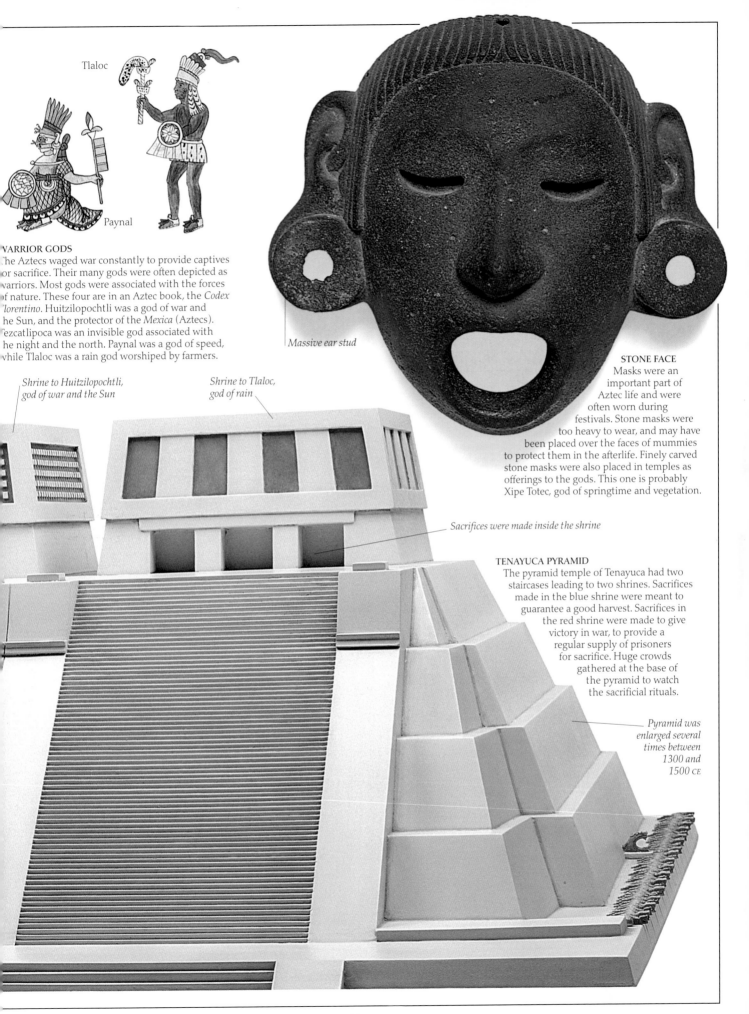

Tlaloc

Paynal

WARRIOR GODS

The Aztecs waged war constantly to provide captives for sacrifice. Their many gods were often depicted as warriors. Most gods were associated with the forces of nature. These four are in an Aztec book, the *Codex Florentino*. Huitzilopochtli was a god of war and the Sun, and the protector of the *Mexica* (Aztecs). Tezcatlipoca was an invisible god associated with the night and the north. Paynal was a god of speed, while Tlaloc was a rain god worshiped by farmers.

Massive ear stud

STONE FACE

Masks were an important part of Aztec life and were often worn during festivals. Stone masks were too heavy to wear, and may have been placed over the faces of mummies to protect them in the afterlife. Finely carved stone masks were also placed in temples as offerings to the gods. This one is probably Xipe Totec, god of springtime and vegetation.

Shrine to Huitzilopochtli, god of war and the Sun

Shrine to Tlaloc, god of rain

Sacrifices were made inside the shrine

TENAYUCA PYRAMID

The pyramid temple of Tenayuca had two staircases leading to two shrines. Sacrifices made in the blue shrine were meant to guarantee a good harvest. Sacrifices in the red shrine were made to give victory in war, to provide a regular supply of prisoners for sacrifice. Huge crowds gathered at the base of the pyramid to watch the sacrificial rituals.

Pyramid was enlarged several times between 1300 and 1500 CE

The pyramid lives on…

Fᴏᴜʀ ᴀɴᴅ ᴀ ʜᴀʟғ ᴛʜᴏᴜsᴀɴᴅ ʏᴇᴀʀs after the Great Pyramid rose on Egypt's desert horizon, a different kind of pyramid is appearing on city skylines. Modern pyramids are not made of millions of tons of stone. It does not take thousands of workers to build them, and they represent big business, not the spiritual realm of the dead. New materials such as reinforced concrete and smoked glass supported by steel girders mean that huge structures can be built with a minimum of effort. There is something special about the pyramid shape that has inspired architects, artists, and designers throughout history. As a geometric shape, it is the supreme symbol of natural balance and harmony. Built on a grand scale, it gives the impression of something superhuman, built by the gods. The eternal magic of the pyramid is destined to live on and on.

THE ROME PYRAMID
The most impressive ancient pyramid in Europe is in Rome. It was built by Caius Cestius, an important official who died in 12 BCE. He is buried beneath the pyramid.

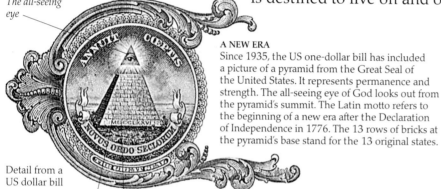

The all-seeing eye

Detail from a US dollar bill

13 rows of bricks symbolizing the 13 original states of the US

Roman numerals for 1776, the year of the Declaration of Independence

A NEW ERA
Since 1935, the US one-dollar bill has included a picture of a pyramid from the Great Seal of the United States. It represents permanence and strength. The all-seeing eye of God looks out from the pyramid's summit. The Latin motto refers to the beginning of a new era after the Declaration of Independence in 1776. The 13 rows of bricks at the pyramid's base stand for the 13 original states.

PYRAMID POWER
This greenhouse is in the botanical gardens in Sydney, Australia. The pyramid shape ensures that a large surface area of glass faces the Sun. But many people believe that the shape itself can generate hidden power or energy. They claim that a blunt razor blade left at the center of a pyramid will be miraculously sharpened!

One-dollar bill from the United States

SETTING THE SCENE
The simple elegance of ancient Egyptian art has inspired many modern artists. The British artist David Hockney designed stage sets for Mozart's opera *The Magic Flute* in 1978. He used the pyramid shape to create a modern sense of grandeur.

A TOMB FOR THE NIGHT

The latest Great Pyramid was not built by a pharaoh of Egypt but by an American businessman, Steve Wynn. It is the Luxor Hotel in Las Vegas, which opened in 1993. It has 5,000 rooms, is 30 stories tall, and cost $300 million to build. The outside is made of black mirrored glass. Before it crouches a replica of the Great Sphinx, even larger than the original, surrounded by plastic palm trees. The fantasy world continues inside the hotel, where a fake Nile River runs through an Egyptian theme park complete with virtual-reality sets and a video-game arcade.

SHAKE-PROOF

Built in 1970, the Transamerica Pyramid in San Francisco rises to a height of 843 ft (257 m). The pyramid shape is part of a special design to combat the deadly shaking of earthquakes, which can topple tall buildings in a few seconds.

REACH FOR THE SKY

The Canary Wharf Tower is the tallest building in Britain. It is topped by a pyramid that dominates the London skyline. The pyramid contains the air-cooling systems and lift machinery for the 50-story skyscraper below it. A flashing light at the tip warns aircraft to keep clear.

The pyramid reflects the old buildings and the sky

Glass is held in place by oxidized steel girders

ides rise at the same ngle as the Great yramid of Giza

ENTERING THE PYRAMID

At the time of the French king Louis XIV (ruled 1643–1715), there were unfulfilled plans to build a pyramid in the grounds of the Louvre palace in Paris. This dream was finally realized three centuries later in 1989, when the Louvre Pyramid was opened by President François Mitterand. The architect I. M. Pei designed it as a new main entrance to the Louvre, which is now a museum. It forms a visitor's reception hall that leads to all the main galleries. Although the modern design was very controversial, because it is surrounded by such historic buildings, it has proved to be very popular.

Did you know?

FASCINATING FACTS

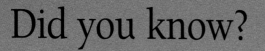

The Great Pyramid of Khufu

Great Pyramid complex at Giza

By the reign of King Tutankhamun (1336–1327 BCE), Khufu's Great Pyramid at Giza (just outside modern-day Cairo) was more than 12 centuries old, and widely visited as a tourist attraction.

Of the Seven Wonders of the Ancient World, the three pyramids at Giza are the oldest, yet they are the only one of these Wonders still in existence.

According to ancient Egyptian hieroglyphic records, fresh garlic was fed to the laborers who were working on the pyramids to keep them strong and healthy.

The pyramids were constructed with incredible accuracy. The foundations of the Great Pyramid, for example, are almost perfectly flat—the highest corner is only ½ in (1.3 cm) above the lowest corner.

The Great Pyramid contains narrow shafts that lead to the outside. Robots carrying cameras explored these shafts in 1993 and 2002. They discovered secret chambers with sealed doors, too small for a person to enter. Further exploration may reveal why the chambers were built, and whether they contain any artifacts.

Centuries of pyramid building and a number of poor harvests seriously harmed Egypt's economy, so pyramids built when the Old Kingdom (c. 2686–2181 BCE) was drawing to a close are much smaller than the earlier pyramids of Khufu and Khafra.

King Amenemhat III (ruled 1855–1808 BCE) built two pyramids. In the first one, at Dahshur, are the tombs of at least three queens, but the pharaoh himself is not buried there; his remains are in his second pyramid at Hawara.

King Amenemhat III

Pyramids built by the Maya of Central America were often painted red, representing their belief that the gods sacrificed their own blood to give humans life.

El Castillo pyramid, Chichén Itzá, Mexico

When the Spanish explorers asked the Aztecs who built the city of Teotihuacan with its two huge pyramids, the Aztecs replied, "the gods."

Ancient Aztec pyramid temple

The architects and engineers of ancient Egypt took 400 years to progress from constructing primitive, flat-topped mastaba tombs to building huge, straight-sided pyramids. The last stage of this process—the leap from stepped to true pyramids—took only 65 years. It constitutes one of the most astonishingly rapid technological advances in history.

One structural factor likely to have influenced the distinctive form of the pyramids is the fact that, before the Romans invented concrete, no other shape could be constructed on such a vast scale, yet still remain strong and stable.

In the early 19th century, a sarcophagus was discovered inside Menkaura's pyramid, but it was lost at sea on its way to the British Museum.

El Castillo was once covered in plaster and red paint

QUESTIONS AND ANSWERS

Q When did we first learn about Egyptian pyramids?

A Worldwide fascination with the tombs of the ancient pharaohs was sparked when French ruler Napoleon Bonaparte's troops visited them during his north African campaign. In 1798, he commissioned a study of Egyptian culture that involved 150 artists, scientists, and engineers, and provided the foundation of our modern knowledge.

The Battle of the Pyramids, by Antoine-Jean Gros

Q What spiritual factors inspired the shape of the pyramids?

A Most straight-sided pyramids are associated with Sun worship, and their sloping sides were intended to echo beams of light. In Egypt, the rising planes also formed a pathway to heaven for the pharaoh's spirit to follow.

Q Have the pyramids at Giza always looked the way they do now?

A No; when the three pyramids were first built, they were surrounded by smaller buildings such as temples, mastaba tombs for important nobles of the court, and small queens' pyramids, in which the pharaohs' wives and other members of the royal family were buried. Also, each pyramid would have been cased in smooth, white limestone that glittered in the Sun.

Q Why are climbers banned from the outer walls of the Giza pyramids?

A Until fairly recently, tourists regularly climbed the Great Pyramid. This caused considerable damage to the overall structure, and also to the individual stones, since people carved or wrote their names on them. In addition, climbers were often injured on the steep sides, and a few even committed suicide by jumping from the top. Since the 1980s, all climbing at the site has been forbidden.

Eiffel Tower,
Paris, France

Q Why did the Aztecs offer human sacrifices on their pyramids?

A The Aztecs worshiped Sun gods and believed that without the constant nourishment of human blood, the Sun would stop shining. Their pyramids were holy places with steep sides reaching up toward the sacred light. On the very top, the nearest place to the Sun, priests would perform bloody sacrificial rites that involved ripping out their victims' still-beating hearts and—on one particular festival—stripping off their skin and wearing it like clothing.

Record breakers

STACKED TOMBS
The first pyramid was built for the Egyptian pharaoh Djoser in about 2650 BCE. Its distinctive stepped shape was a result of its simple construction: a number of flat, rectangular mastaba tombs of decreasing size stacked on top of one another.

SUPER STRUCTURE
The Great Pyramid at Giza is not only the largest pyramid in the world, but, 44 centuries after it was built, it is still the largest burial monument and the largest stone structure ever made.

STANDING TALL
Until tall cathedral spires were erected in the late Middle Ages, the Great Pyramid was the tallest structure in existence.

LIFE'S WORK
Khufu's father, Sneferu, built at least three, maybe more, pyramids. Although none of them was as big as his son's monument, together they represented an even more extensive construction project.

SOLID STONE
When it was finished, the Great Pyramid contained more stone than all the cathedrals of modern Europe existing today. The main structure contained approximately 2.3 million blocks, weighing an average of 2.8 tons (2.5 metric tons) each. The largest stones weighed about 55 tons (50 metric tons).

SACRED LIST
Among the earliest existing writings on papyrus are fragments of a list kept by scribes of all the offerings made at the pyramid temple of King Neferirkara (ruled 2475–2455 BCE).

EARLY EXPLORATIONS
The first excavations at the Giza pyramids were made by King Thutmosis IV in about 1400 BCE.

TALL, TALLER, TALLEST
Although it was the tallest of all the Aztec pyramids, the Great Temple at Tenochtitlan was only one-fifth as tall as Khufu's Great Pyramid.

WRITING ON THE WALLS
The oldest known religious writings are sacred hieroglyphs called the Pyramid Texts. Dating from about 2340 BCE, they were found on the walls of some of the chambers inside the pyramid of King Unas.

The Pyramid Texts in the tomb of King Unas

King Djoser

Who's who?

THE PYRAMIDS OF THE ANCIENT WORLD were built on a scale so massive and overwhelming that it is easy to forget that the extraordinary power, skill, and sheer strength behind them came from ordinary people. We know very little about the laborers who actually built these awesome monuments, nor, in most cases, can we identify the architects and engineers who designed them. What we do have, however, is a fascinating record of many of the ancient rulers who commissioned them.

PYRAMID BUILDERS

The Pyramid Texts in Unas's tomb

DJOSER

Third-Dynasty king who built the first pyramid in about 2650 BCE. Stepped in structure, Djoser's historic tomb at Saqqara was the model for all the Egyptian pyramids that followed. His architect, the high priest Imhotep, pioneered the use of stone rather than mud brick for building.

SNEFURU

Fourth-Dynasty pharaoh who built several pyramids for himself and his family, including the first example with smooth, as opposed to stepped, sides. Snefuru was the father of Khufu.

KHUFU

Sometimes known by his Greek name, Cheops, Khufu commissioned the largest tomb of all, the Great Pyramid, on the west bank of the Nile at Giza, about 2589 BCE.

Hieroglyphs from King Sahura's pyramid

KHAFRA

Thought to be Khufu's son— or possibly his younger brother— Khafra built the second Giza pyramid. Although smaller than Khufu's, it looks taller since it is built on higher ground and its summit is still intact.

MENKAURA

Builder of the third, and smallest, Giza pyramid, Menkaura is believed to be Khafra's son. South of his pyramid, he placed three smaller queens' pyramids for his wives and children.

SAHURA

Earliest 5th-Dynasty king to be buried in a complex of pyramids at Abusir, south of Giza. Sahura's tomb is the best preserved at this site, and the only one open to visitors. Nearby is the pyramid of his brother and heir, Neferirkara, which is about the same size as Menkaura's at Giza.

UNAS

Final pharaoh of the Fifth Dynasty, Unas built his pyramid at the Saqqara complex. Today, his tomb is best known for the important hieroglyphic writings (called the Pyramid Texts) discovered on the walls of the burial chamber.

Rekhmire's tomb drawings

PEPY I AND II

Sixth-Dynasty pharaohs whose comparatively small pyramids at Saqqara were the last to be built for more than 200 years.

AMENEMHAT I

The first king of the Middle Kingdom (2055–1650 BCE) to construct a true pyramid. It was located at Lisht. Like all pyramids built during this era, Amenemhat I's pyramid was smaller and less well-constructed than those of the Old Kingdom (c. 2686–2181 BCE).

REKHMIRE

An official during the reigns of Thutmosis III and Amenhotep II, Rekhmire was buried in a tomb that contained fascinating wall drawings illustrating details of pyramid construction.

THUTMOSIS IV

Eighteenth-Dynasty king who undertook early explorations of the Giza pyramids about 1400 BCE. Thutmosis also made one of the first attempts to free the Sphinx from the drifting sands that had buried the figure up to its neck.

TAHARQO

Nubian king who ruled over both Nubia and Egypt during the 25th Dynasty. Inspired by the Giza pyramids, Taharqo's huge monument at Nuri was one of 20 kings' pyramids and 53 queens' pyramids at the site.

AMANISHAKHETO

Nubian queen during the 1st century BCE whose pyramid, uniquely, was still full of treasures in the early 19th century.

PYRAMID EXPLORERS

THE KNOWLEDGE WE HAVE about the pyramids came to us largely through the efforts of intrepid explorers, archeologists, and historians of many nationalities who devoted their lives to uncovering the secrets of the pyramids.

Golden necklace from the pyramid of Queen Amanishakheto

HERODOTUS

Greek historian who drew up one of the earliest accounts (c. 450 BCE) of how the pyramids were constructed. Later, some of his theories were disproved.

Herodotus

NAPOLEON BONAPARTE

After he invaded Egypt in 1798, the French general Napoleon Bonaparte (later emperor of France) commissioned the first modern study of Egypt's ancient culture.

LUIGI MAYER

Italian adventurer whose illustrated volume *Views in Egypt* (published 1804) helped stimulate interest in Egypt's history.

JEAN-FRANÇOIS CHAMPOLLION

French scholar, linguist, and archeologist responsible for the single largest contribution to Egyptology ever made: the deciphering of ancient hieroglyphics in 1822.

GIUSEPPE FERLINI

A notable villain in the history of Egyptology, Ferlini discovered a hoard of jewelry in Queen Amanishakheto's miraculously preserved pyramid in 1834. In his search for further riches, he damaged the structure irrevocably.

HOWARD VYSE

Author of one of the earliest and most famous reference books on the pyramids, *The Pyramids of Gizeh*, published in 1837.

W. M. FLINDERS PETRIE

English archeologist who made the first detailed study of the Giza pyramids in 1881–82. Petrie also published more than 1,000 books and papers and pioneered several techniques for pyramid exploration.

JEAN-PHILIPPE LAUER

Twentieth-century French architect and Egyptologist who devoted his life to reconstructing the Step Pyramid at Saqqara.

Jean-Philippe Lauer

FREDERICK CATHERWOOD AND JOHN LLOYD STEPHENS

Mid-19th-century explorers who discovered a number of ancient Mayan ruins in the Mexican jungle. Englishman Catherwood produced some of the first widely seen sketches of the distinctive pyramids of Central America. Stephens, an American, recorded their pioneering discoveries in two volumes of published diaries, which he called *Incidents of Travel*.

W. M. Flinders Petrie

AUGUSTE MARIETTE

Nineteenth-century French Egyptologist who discovered Khafra's Valley Temple at Giza and the Serapeum (burial chamber for sacred bulls) at Saqqara. Mariette went on to found the original Egyptian Museum at Cairo.

Mayan pyramid, 19-century illustration from Catherwood and Stephens' *Incidents of Travel*

Find out more

THE WEALTH OF TREASURES unearthed from ancient pyramids has made it possible for museums all over the world to put together collections of objects and artworks that communicate some of the magic of these ancient structures. There is also a wealth of printed material available. While you can readily find information on all the pyramids in Egypt and in Central America, the focus of much of the available material is the Giza plateau, with its legendary Old Kingdom pyramids. Dominated by the Great Pyramid and the Sphinx, the Giza complex once also contained temples, mastaba tombs, smaller pyramids, and covered causeways. Today, it is surrounded by tourists, yet the immense structures still make a powerful impression on those who visit them.

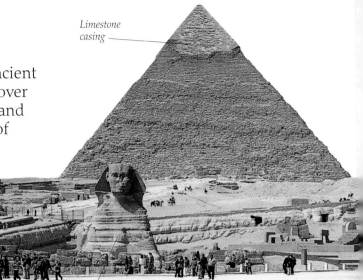

Limestone casing

Sphinx has the body of a lion and the head of a man

Crumbled ruins of the pyramid of King Unas

ETERNAL WATCH
Guarded by its Sphinx, whose face was carved in the pharaoh's image, Khafra's pyramid is the only one that retains—at its tip—some of the limestone casing that originally covered all three tombs. The rest was removed by medieval rulers of Cairo, who used it for their own monuments. This is the view of the complex from the edge of the Giza Plateau.

The Great Pyramid of Khufu

RUINED MONUMENT
Just south of the enclosure walls at Saqqara is the ruined pyramid of King Unas, who ruled Egypt from about 2375 to 2345 BCE. The entire Saqqara burial site, which is south of Cairo near Memphis, originally extended for more than 4 miles (7 km) from north to south.

IN HIS MASTER'S SHADOW
It was not only pharaohs and their families who were buried on the Giza plateau; important members of the royal household could also be laid to rest there. This tomb, with its starkly beautiful columns guarding the entrance, was built for Seshemnufer, one of Khufu's courtiers.

USEFUL WEBSITES

USEFUL WEBSITES

- Take the Pyramid Challenge and see if you could be a pyramid builder at this detailed website on ancient Egypt: www.bbc.co.uk/history/ancient/egyptians
- Children's history site relating to the culture of ancient Egypt: www.historyforkids.org/learn/egypt/
- Specialized Egyptian site run by the British Museum: www.ancientegypt.co.uk
- Excellent in-depth website on Egyptian pyramids: www.guardians.net/egypt/pyramids.htm
- The Met's Egyptian Art page, with links to special features: www.metmuseum.org/work_of_art/egyptian_art/
- General introduction to pyramids, with plenty of links to other sites: http://science.howstuffworks.com/pyramid.htm

Lotus-adorned Egyptian vessel in the British Museum

KUKULCAN'S CASTLE
El Castillo (The Castle), at Chichén Itzá in Mexico, was built in around 800 CE and dedicated to Kukulcan, the Mayan version of the ancient god Quetzalcoatl. Overall, the pyramid is 79 ft (24 m) high; the square structure at the very top is Kukulcan's temple.

TRICKS OF THE LIGHT
At the foot of El Castillo's north staircase are two serpents' heads, thought to represent the god Kukulcan himself. At both equinoxes, the play of light on the staircase makes it look as if these sacred creatures are crawling down the pyramid's steep facade.

TOOLS OF THE TRADE
Many of the implements used by ancient Egyptian pyramid builders are strikingly similar to their modern equivalents. Then, as now, a carpenter's saw cut through lumber, while his chisel was used for detailed work such as carving images and hieroglyphs. The examples below are both models discovered in the foundations of Thutmosis III's temple.

Chisel

Saw

Places to visit

GIZA PYRAMIDS, CAIRO, EGYPT
In the interest of preservation, and in order for necessary restoration to be done, the three pyramids are closed alternately to tourists. Some of the best sites to see are:
- the Great Gallery and the King's Chamber in the Great Pyramid of Khufu
- the Solar Boat Museum, which exhibits a full-sized boat discovered—in pieces—in a pit beside the Great Pyramid
- the remains of the mortuary temple, sanctuary, and courtyard outside King Khafra's tomb

SAQQARA, NEAR MEMPHIS, EGYPT
Necropolis (burial ground) of the Old Kingdom capital of Memphis, Saqqara is one of the most important archeological sites in Egypt. Among its treasures are:
- the step pyramid of King Djoser, prototype for all Egyptian pyramids
- the pyramid of the last Fifth-Dynasty king, Unas, which contains the important hieroglyphic inscriptions known as the Pyramid Texts

METROPOLITAN MUSEUM OF ART, NEW YORK, NY
The Met's collection of ancient Egyptian art is among the finest outside of Egypt. With thousands of objects on display in 32 major galleries, visitors can learn about every aspect and era of this ancient culture. Of particular interest are:
- the mastaba of Perneb, a restored tomb from the Age of the Pyramids
- a Middle Kingdom coffin, covered in hieroglyphic text and decorative panels

CAHOKIA MOUNDS, COLLINSVILLE, IL
This site was once the regional center of the Mississippian culture, one of the most advanced prehistoric civilizations in the United States. Visitors can see:
- 80 preserved earthen mounds or pyramids
- an interpretive center with artifacts from the site
- Monks Mound, the largest prehistoric earthen mound in the country

EL CASTILLO, CHICHÉN ITZÁ, MEXICO
Built around 800 CE, this Mayan temple dominates the Chichén Itzá site and affords a stunning view of the surrounding countryside. Visitors can see:
- the serpents' heads at the bottom of the north staircase, which are believed to represent the god Kukulcan, the Mayan version of the Aztec god Quetzalcoatl
- the temple at the top of the inner pyramid

PYRAMIDS OF THE SUN AND MOON, TEOTIHUACAN, MEXICO
Completed in the 2nd century CE, these stepped pyramids are made of sun-dried mud bricks and earth, faced with gravel and stone. Worth investigating are:
- the on-site museum, which displays a scale model of the ancient city
- the view from the top of the Pyramid of the Moon

Glossary

Adze

ADZE Ancient Egyptian tool for carving and planing wood.

ANCIENT EGYPT The period when Egypt was ruled by pharaohs, which was between around 3100 BCE and 30 BCE.

ANKH Ancient Egyptian symbol of life that, traditionally, only gods and royalty carried.

ANTECHAMBER Small room that leads to a bigger or more important one.

ARTIFACT Ancient man-made object usually unearthed during archeological explorations.

AZTECS Central American civilization that dominated Mexico before the Spanish conquest in the 16th century.

BONING RODS Pair of cylinders joined by a length of string, and used to establish a smooth, flat surface on the stone sides of a true pyramid.

Capital

CAPITAL The top section of an architectural column, which in ancient Egypt was often shaped like a locally growing plant, such as palm or papyrus leaves or lotus flowers.

Ancient Egyptian frieze

CAPSTONE Finishing (topmost) stone on top of a pyramid or wall.

CARTOUCHE In Egyptology, an oval border enclosing a pharaoh's name in hieroglyphics.

CASING Outer covering layer of smooth, fine stone on a building.

CATARACT Powerful rush of water around a large rock that blocks a river's flow. Important monuments were often sited near cataracts on the Nile River.

CAUSEWAY Raised road across a low or wet area of ground or a body of water.

CENOTAPH Memorial monument to a person or a group of people buried elsewhere.

CODICES Ancient manuscript texts in book form.

COLONNADE Row of architectural columns supporting arches or a decorative upper surface.

CONQUISTADORS Spanish invaders who plundered Central and South America in the 16th century.

CUBIT Unit of measurement in ancient Egypt, roughly equal to the length from the elbow to the tip of the thumb (20½ in or 52.4 cm). A cubit was divided into seven palms, and each palm into four digits.

DOLERITE Extremely hard, coarse rock.

DYNASTY Series of rulers belonging to the same family. There were about 30 dynasties during the history of ancient Egypt.

FRIEZE Broad horizontal band of decoration on a wall.

GLYPHS Pictorial images used to represent words by the Maya people of Central America.

HIEROGLYPHS Picture writing used to build up words in ancient Egyptian script.

INCAS Civilization that flourished in Peru before the 16th-century Spanish conquest.

KHAT Baglike cover worn over a pharaoh's wig.

LABYRINTH Intricate and confusing network of passages.

LAPIS LAZULI Bright blue semiprecious stone commonly found in Egyptian jewelry and artifacts.

Model of a *conquistador* on horseback and a foot soldier

LOTUS Water lily whose shape was widely used as a decorative device in ancient Egypt.

MASTABA Early Egyptian tomb, made of sun-dried mud bricks and stone. Mastabas are oblong, with low, sloping sides and a flat roof.

MAYA Advanced Central American culture that collapsed during the 800s. The Mayan people were renowned pyramid builders.

MIDDLE KINGDOM The period of ancient Egyptian history from 2055 to 1650 BCE.

MUMMY Dead body that has been preserved from decay, either naturally or by artificial means.

NEW KINGDOM The period of ancient Egyptian history from 1550 to 1069 BCE.

NICHE Shallow recess in a wall intended for display or storage. The Pyramid of the Niches in Mexico has 365 recesses, which may have held religious figures or offerings to the gods.

OBELISK Tapered stone column with a square or rectangular base and sloping sides rising to a pointed tip.

OBSIDIAN Glassy rock formed from solidified lava used for decoration and as a mirror. Because obsidian forms an extremely sharp edge when it breaks, it was also used to make cutting implements.

OLD KINGDOM The period of ancient Egyptian history from about 2686 to 2181 BCE.

OSTRACON Fragment of stone or pottery inscribed with writing or drawing.

PALETTE Flat surface on which colors were mixed to make either writing pigments or cosmetics.

PAPYRUS Tall riverside reed whose stem was widely used to make baskets, boats, sandals, rope, and paperlike sheets or scrolls for writing on.

The Living Pharaoh (Ramses II), by Winifred Brunton, 1920s

PHARAOH Title given to the rulers of ancient Egypt. The word pharaoh means "great house," and originally referred to the palace rather than the king.

PLAZA Open square or market place in a town or city.

PYRAMID Massive stone structure with a square base and sloping sides, which can be either straight or stepped. In ancient societies, pyramids were usually built as tombs, temples, or monuments.

PYRAMIDION Conelike capstone for the pointed roof of a scaled-down, pyramid-shaped tomb. These small brick structures were popular long after full-sized pyramids had fallen out of favor.

QUARRY Site where stone is extracted from the ground to be used for buildings, monuments, or sculptures.

QUEEN'S PYRAMID Small pyramid built near a major one to contain the remains of a pharaoh's wives and children, or to fulfill an unknown symbolic function.

SARCOPHAGUS Elaborate outer coffin made of stone.

SACRIFICE The killing of people or animals as part of a religious ceremony. The Aztecs sacrificed people to the gods on top of their Great Pyramid.

SCHIST Layered rock, made up of sheets of different minerals, that splits into thin, irregular plates.

SCRIBE Government official who, unlike most ordinary people, could read and write.

SED **COURT** Elongated rectangular space in the step pyramid complexes where, watched by assembled crowds, pharaohs would traditionally run a course to show their fitness.

SEKED Ancient Egyptian term referring to the angle of a pyramid's sloping sides.

SERDAB Small chamber in a tomb intended to contain a statue of the deceased, which his or her spirit could inhabit after death.

SHABTIS Figures made in the image of servants and often buried with important people so they could perform any manual tasks that were required in the afterlife. The word *shabti* comes from an Egyptian term meaning "to answer."

SLED Vehicle on runners designed to carry heavy loads. When the pyramids were under construction, the building materials and stone blocks were transported to the sites on sleds.

SLIPWAY Artificial slope constructed beside a pyramid building site, on which men and equipment could be transported.

SOUL HOUSE Miniature model dwelling placed in the tomb of its dead owner for his or her use in the afterlife.

SPHINX In ancient Egypt, the sphinx was a monumental creature with a lion's body and the head of the ruler. Sphinxes were a symbol of royal power. They were believed to guard the entrances to the underworld on both the east and the west horizons.

STELA Upright stone slab or pillar covered with carvings or inscriptions.

STUCCO Durable, slow-setting plaster used as an outer covering on buildings or pieces of pottery.

TERRACE Raised level space near a building or in a garden, designed for walking or standing.

Tomb of the noble Seshemnufer, in the shadow of the Great Pyramid

TOBE Egyptian word for brick; also the root of the modern word adobe, meaning a sun-dried brick, or a style of architecture that uses this building material.

TOLTECS Warlike people who inhabited Mexico before and during the time of the Aztecs. The Toltecs were also pyramid builders, and they are suspected of introducing their pyramid rituals of human sacrifice to the Maya.

TOMB Grave, monument, or building where the body of a dead person is laid to rest.

VIZIERS The highest officials in ancient Egypt, who were appointed by the pharaoh to rule over Upper and Lower Egypt.

WEDJET (*WADJET*) **EYE** Protective symbol widely used in ancient Egypt, which represents the eye of the sky-god Horus. Also known as the Eye of Horus.

Great Stela at Axum

Index

A

Abu Roash 9
Abusir 24, 38, 69
Abydos 29
Amanishakheto, Queen 52–53, 66, 67
Amenemhat I 40, 66
Amenemhat III 40, 42, 43, 64
Amenhotep 33
Amun 26, 41, 52, 53
Anherkhau 34
Anlamani 50
Anubis 45
Apedemak 53
Aspelta 50
Aswan 32, 43
Atet 15
Axumites 48
Aztecs 6, 54, 60–61, 64, 65

BC

basalt 24, 32
Belize 54, 56
Belzoni, Giovanni, 22
Bent Pyramid 8, 14, 15, 21
Bersha 46
Black Pyramid 42
boats, funeral 28–29
boats, reed 28
Bonampak 59
boning rods 30
Book of the Dead 22, 29, 44, 50
bricks 33, 40
Brunton, Winifred 39, 42, 43, 51
Bugentef 44
building pyramids 32–37, 64, 66, 69
Cairo 6, 7, 20, 21, 64, 69
Campeche 56
Canary Wharf Tower 63
capstones 43, 44–45
cartouches 18, 32–33, 34, 40, 42, 43, 50
casing 32, 36, 68, 70
Catherwood, Frederick 59, 67
Caviglia, Giovanni 27
Central America 6, 54–61
Cestius, Caius 62
Champollion, Jean-François 46, 67

Cheops *see* Khufu
Chichén Itzá 6, 56, 57, 64, 69
Cocijo 55
Codex Florentino 61
conquistadors 54, 60
cubits 30

DE

Dahshur 14, 40, 42, 47, 64
Deir el-Bahri 35, 41
Dixon, Waynman 46
Djehutyhotep 46
Djoser 7, 10–13, 42, 65, 66
dolerite 34
dollar bills 62
dummy buildings 12, 13
Edfu temple 31
El Castillo 56, 57, 64, 69
El Lahun 40, 42
El Salvador 56
El Tajín 55
Eye of Horus 28, 52

FG

Ferlini, Giuseppe 52, 67
Flinders Petrie, W. M. 14, 18, 67
foundations 30, 31, 50, 64
funerals 24
Gebel Barkal 48, 53
Giza 6, 16–21, 26–27, 50, 64, 65, 66, 67, 68–69
glyphs 56–57, 58–59
granite 32, 34
Great Pyramid 14, 16–17, 20–21, 54, 64, 65, 68, 69;
  construction 20, 32, 36, 64;
  entrance 22;
  explorers 23;
  Grand Gallery 22, 23;
  King's Chamber 20, 23, 32;
  layout 23;
  mortuary temples 24;
  names 18;
  planning 30;
  Queen's Chamber 23;
  ventilation shafts 23, 46, 47, 64
Guatemala 56, 58, 59

H

Hatshepsut, Queen 41
Hawara 43, 64
Heh 48

Heliopolis 44, 45
Herodotus 36, 67
Hesire 31
Hetepheres 9, 47
hieroglyphs 18, 38, 46, 67
Hockney, David 62
Honduras 56
Horemakhet 27
Horus 18, 27, 28, 38, 52
human sacrifices 6, 54, 58, 60
Hunefer 29, 44

IJK

Imhotep 10, 11, 13, 66
Ipi 32
Java 6
jewelry 40, 42, 43, 52–53, 67
Kagemni 28
Karnak 26, 41
Katep 9
Khaem-waset 32
Khafra 6, 16–19, 26–27, 66, 68
Khamerernebty 19
Khufu 14, 16–19, 20, 21, 23, 28, 29, 64, 66
Kukulcan 69
Kurru 48

LM

La Venta 54
laborers 8, 36, 46
Las Vegas 63
Lauer, Jean-Philippe 12, 67
limestone 32
Lisht 8, 40, 66
Lost Pyramid 46
Louvre Pyramid 63
Luxor 26
Maat 45
Maghara 14
Ma'mun, Caliph 22
Mariette, Auguste 67
masks 54, 61
masons 30, 34
mastabas 7, 10, 41, 64, 65
Mayan people 6, 54, 56–59, 64, 67, 69
Mayer, Luigi 17, 67
Meidum pyramid 7, 14–15, 32
Memphis 8, 13, 18, 41, 50, 68, 69
Menkaura 16–19, 33, 64, 66
Mentuhotep 41

Mereret 42, 43
Mereruka 10
Merib 25
Meroe 44, 48, 52–53
Mexico 6, 54–55, 56, 58, 64, 67, 69
Middle Kingdom 6, 8, 40–41
Moche people 54
models, 30, 35
mortuary temples 24–25, 39
mummies 24, 44
Mut 52

N

Napata 48
Napoleon I, Emperor 23, 65, 67
Nawidamak, Queen 52
necropolis 69
Nefer Maat 15
Neferirkara 38, 65, 66, 69
Nefertiabet 25
Neith 39
New Kingdom 6, 44
Nile River 7, 8, 16, 28, 30, 32, 43
Nofret 14
Nubia 26, 41, 42, 45, 48–53, 66
Nuri 48, 50, 51, 66
Nyuserra 38, 69

O

oars 28
offerings 24–25
officials 8
Old Kingdom 6, 8, 39, 40
Olmecs 54
Orion 47
Osiris 29, 32
ostraca 32

P

paintings 15, 24–25, 33, 34, 41, 56
papyrus 31, 32, 39, 65
Pei, I. M. 63
Pepy I 39, 66
Pepy II 39, 66
Peru 54
pharaohs 8–9, 18–19, 50–51
shabti figures 50, 51
Sinai Peninsula 14, 21
sleds 37, 46
Sneferu 14–15, 47, 65, 66
Piazzi Smyth, Charles 47
planning pyramids 30–31

Ptah 11, 32
Pyramid of the Giant Jaguar 58, 59
Pyramid of the Magician 58
Pyramid of the Moon 69
Pyramid of the Niches 55
Pyramid of the Sun 54, 69
Pyramid Texts 7, 22, 47, 65, 66
pyramidions 44–45

QR

quarries 32
queens' pyramids 16, 17, 19, 21, 51, 65, 66
Quetzalcoatl 56, 57, 60
Radjedef 9, 29
Rahotep 14
ramps 36–37
Ramses II 32
Raneferef 38, 69
Re 7, 28, 39, 44, 45, 47
Rekhmire 30, 33, 34, 36, 66
Rhind Papyrus 30
Rivera, Diego 55
robbers 25, 38, 40, 43
Rome 62
Rosetta Stone 32

S

sacrifices 6, 54, 58, 60, 64, 65
Sahura 38, 39, 66, 69
sandstone 32, 51
Saqqara 10–13, 28, 32, 39, 46, 66, 67, 68, 69
sarcophagus 22
Sat-Hathor III 40
scaffolding 34
scribes 31
sed court 12, 13, 41, 71,
Sekhemket 46
Senkamanisken 51
Sennedjsui 25
Senusret I 40
Senusret II 40
Senusret III 28, 42
Serapeum 67
servants 8, 9
Seshemnufer 24
Seven Wonders of the Ancient World 21, 64

T

Taharqo 50–51, 66
Takhenmes 47
Temple of Siva 6
temples 24–25, 38, 39, 54, 56, 65
Tenayuca pyramid 61
Tenochtitlán 60, 65
Teotihuacan 54, 69
Thebes 41
Thoth 21
Ti 24
Tikal 58, 59
Toltecs 56, 57, 58
tools 30, 34–35, 46, 60, 69
Transamerica Pyramid 63
treasures 22
Tulum 59
Tura 32, 38
Tutankhamun 22, 64, 69
Tuthmosis III 35, 69
Tuthmosis IV 26, 27, 49, 49, 65, 66, 69
Twain, Mark 20

U–Z

Udjahor 45
Unas 22, 32, 65, 66, 68
United States 62, 63
Userkaf 38, 39
Uxmal, 58
Valley of the Kings 22
  ventilation shafts 23, 46, 47
Vyse, Howard 38
wedjet eye 28, 52
writing 22, 46, 56–57, 58, 59
Wynn, Steve 63
Yucatán Peninsula 54, 56
Zapotecs 54, 55

South America 54
Spain 54, 60
Sphinx 6, 16, 18, 26–27, 63, 66, 68
stars 47
statues 9, 11
stelae 25, 44
Step Pyramid 10–13, 42, 65, 66, 69
step pyramids 7, 14, 47
Stephens, John Lloyd 59, 67
stone 32, 34, 66
Sudan 6, 44, 48
Sun 6, 7, 38, 47, 57
Sun worship 65
Sydney 62

Acknowledgments

Dorling Kindersley would like to thank:
The staff of the Department of Egyptian Antiquities, British Museum, London, in particular John Taylor, Stephen Quirke, Carol Andrews, Jeffrey Spencer, Virginia Hewitt, Tony Brandon, Bob Dominey, and John Hayman; the British Museum Photographic Department, especially Ivor Kerslake; Angela Thomas and Arthur Boulton at the Bolton Museum; Robert Bauval; Jean-Phillipe Lauer; Helena Spiteri, and Linda Martin for editorial help; Sharon Spencer, Susan St. Louis, Isaac Zamora, and Ivan Finnegan for design help; Sarah Owens for proofreading; Hilary Bird for the index; Peter Radcliffe and Steve Setford for the wallchart; and Jo Mitchell, Sue Malyan, and Jessamy Wood for the clipart CD.

Additional photography by Peter Anderson (25ar, 36–37, 41br, 47l), Stan Bean (12–13), Janet Peckham (46cr), Dave Rudkin (55b), Karl Shone.
Maps by Simone End (6cr, 8r, 54c)
Illustrations by John Woodcock (18bl, 21t, 41c, 54br), Sergio Momo (54c)

The Publishers would like to thank the following for their kind permission to reproduce their photographs:

(Key: a-above; b-below/bottom; c-center; f-far; l-left; r-right; t-top)

Ayeshah Abdel-Haleem: 22br; Ancient Art and Architecture Collection: 37ar, 41ar; Stan Bean / Egyptian Museum, San José, Ca: 12–13b; Biblioteca Medicea Laurenziania / Photo - Scardigli: 60ar, 61al; Phot. Bibl. Nat., Paris / Codex Telleriano-Remensis: 61cl; The Ancient Egypt Picture Library: Robert Partridge 65tc; Bibliothèque du Musée de l'Homme: 57ac; British Museum: 67ac; J.Allan Cash Photolibrary: 62cr; J.L.Charmet: 59cl; G. Dagli Orti: 59ar; Vivien Davis: 48cl, 48–49b; e.t.archive: 7c, 22cl, (detail) 43bl, 55ar; Mary Evans Picture Library: 16al, 17cr, 20bl, 22al, 47c, 60c; Francis Firth/Royal Photographic Society, Bath (The southern stone pyramid of Dahshoor from the south west): 14cr; Gallimard Jeunesse:

17ar, 18c; Robert Harding Picture Library: 47br, 63al, 63ar; Gavin Hellier: 64cra; © David Hockney/ Photo-Guy Gravett: 62bl; Hutchison Library: 6bl, 58cl / Pate, 6ar, 57ar; Image Bank / Luis Castañeda: 58ac / Derek Berwin: 63cl. INAH: 57al; H. Lewandowski / Photo - R.M.N.: 9al; Jürgen Liepe: 11br, 18al, 18cr, 38br, 39cl, 46cl; Mansell Collection: (detail) 21bcr, 37cr, 38cl; © Metropolitan Museum of Art, Gift of Edward S. Harkness, 1914 (14.3.17): 40l; Daniel Moignot, P.L.J. Gallimard-Larousse: 37al; Museum Expedition. Courtesy of Museum of Fine Arts, Boston: 19r; National Palace, Mexico City / Photo—e.t. archive (detail, Diego Rivera "Totonac Civilisation")— Reproduction authorizada por el Instituto Nacional de Bellas Artes y Literatura: 55al; James Putnam: 7cr, 17al, 19al, 20ar, 21c, 42cl, 43cl, 51ac; R.M.N: 25br; John Ross: 12al; Royal Museum of Scotland: 56bl; Royal Observatory, Edinburgh: 47 ar; John Sandford/Science Photo Library: 47acr; Staatliche Museen zu Berlin Preussischer Kulturbesitz Agyptisches Museum / Photo—Margarete Busing / Bildarchiv: 52ar, 52b, 52c, 53a, 53b, 53br; Tony Stone Images: 63bc; Werner Forman Archive: 14ar, 15al, 22bl, 31cl, 32cr, (detail) 35cl, (detail)

35ac, 39ar; Michel Zabé: 56–57b, 57cr, 58–59b, 60–61b; Zefa: 54bl / J. Schörken, 56al.

Wallchart:

Ancient Art & Architecture Collection: Ronald Sheridan ca (workers); DK Images: Bolton Metro Museum clb (hieroglyph), fcrb; British Museum ca (chisel), cla (mallet), crb (good luck charm), fcla; Cairo Museum cra (both statues); © CONACULTA-INAH-MEX. Authorized reproduction by the Instituto Nacional de Antropologia e Historia bc, bl; Michel Zabé bc (human sacrifice); Getty Images: Gianluigi Guercia / AFP cb (pyramids of Nubia)

Jacket:
Front: Corbis: Danny Lehman tc. **Dorling Kindersley:** The British Museum tl, tr. Getty Images: Stone / Will & Denny Macintyre b. *Back:* Dorling Kindersley: Bolton Metro Museum cla (hieroglyphics); The British Museum bl, c, cr (adze), cr (saw), crb, cra, tl. Jürgen Liepe: cl, tr.

All other images © Dorling Kindersley.
For further information see:
www.dkimages.com